GW00777490

Advance Reade. .˷˓˷˓˷˓
and Personal Reflections.

*"I was raised in Northern Ireland during '**The Troubles**'. Considered to be "the norm" by many, there was nothing normal about growing up during a sectarian war. Many of us who survived this brutally dark period of Ireland's history, including me, now live with undiagnosed effects of Post-Traumatic Stress Disorder (PTSD). I refuse to let this define who I am or for it to cloud my worldview.*

Although I am Irish, I follow holistic practices taught to me by Cree and Anishinaabe peoples. A Cree Elder said:

"Be careful with what words you say. Once you put them out to the universe, you can never take them back."

My role as a social worker is to assist people to navigate their way through various forms of abuse and trauma. Please note this book may trigger old, perhaps suppressed emotions of your own personal experiences. If this is indeed the case and you require counselling, understand you are not alone. Contact the mental health center in your community. Asking for help is the first step to healing. Take each day one step at a time. And remember to breathe!"

- **Greg McVicker, BSW.**
  Irish Author and Poet.

"The author managed to capture the emancipation of one women's experience after being trapped in a one-sided, loveless marriage. Unfortunately, this is not an isolated or unique story. The constant crushing of her hopes and dreams for a loving relationship as her parents had were shattered time and time again, which left her mourning the loss of the children and life she dreamt. Everyone has problems, and marriage is meant to be the union of two souls coming together to support and unite against what life throws at you. Instead, this story shows the strength of character of this woman and the many others who break the cycle of abuse, especially after the constant degrading verbal abuse suffered by the tongue of a man who is so weak of character that he can only feel strong when making another human being feel so low, and downtrodden.

A heartfelt account which gives strength in the union of survival, empowering the next generation to be aware of the signs of potential patterns of abuse and develop the strength needed to stand tall and strong in life."

- **Christina Moffett**
  Belfast, Northern Ireland.

"Five stars!

This book is extremely emotional, heart-rendering and gut-wrenching. It certainly draws you into the story of a woman who has been mentally abused over many years in her marriage. The mental torture and mind-gruelling name calling will bring a lump to your throat or a punch of anger to sit heavily in your stomach. No woman, regardless of race, gender or sex, should ever have to endure what this woman did. I applaud her for not only trying her hardest to make the marriage work but sticking at it for as long as she did in hopes of life getting better.

I was definitely sent on a rollercoaster adventure of emotions and found myself close to tears in more than one place. It's a gritty and nervy read, with the right amount of emotion. And the writing style was incredible in drawing the reader in and keeping them there. There's statistics within the book that will make you gasp; the level-percentage of abusive relationships is rather astonishing.

The poems that can be read at the end of the story are very well written, and visually effective. As well as the author's words at the end about writing the book along with the anonymous woman behind the words, was good to read too.

Gritty. Nervy. Emotional and full of anguish, this is a story that needs to be read. It can be a trigger to women out there, but I believe it could also help women see that there is another side, one without the abuse.

Fabulously written."

- **L. Grubb**
  Southampton, United Kingdom.
  Author of the best-selling 'Crusaders MC' series.

"I would like to thank you for letting me read this. The impact was very powerful. I felt like I was living it through her. I really could not put it down. It was a very difficult subject that was written extremely well to make me understand what some have to endure to survive and just how fortunate I am."

- **Liz Havercost**
  Alberta, Canada.

*"As a wonderfully written book, with such an unfortunate base. I am so glad she escaped. The emotional abuse takes such a horrible toll on one's mind and soul. It bears an eerily familiarity to my own story when I was younger. And many friends of mine too, sadly. Thankfully I am now an **#iwas**, and not an **#iam**."*

- **Jaime Knight**
  Manitoba, Canada.

"It is not life threatening when someone is screaming at you. At least they aren't hitting you."

"I have endured the forty questions every time you leave and come home, sitting in fear as you are interrogated, wondering if today the words I chose will be the right ones, or will I manage not to blink too much. I fell down the rabbit hole of 'her' story and I walked beside 'her' through each word. Every time I read "my ex" my heart squeezed in triumph for us all, it screams of a strength louder than the battle cries of old. By the end, I could see those brown eyes, I could see into her hell. I cried with frustration and anger, I reveled in her triumphs, her rebellions and her strength. Her story is one of immense pain, but her spirit shines through. I am her, she is me. Thank you for giving us a voice.

I'm sure I could use better language in my descriptions of feelings. I've been highlighting my favourite passages as I go, it truly is a soulful read. I want to smash the fucker round the head with an iron but that's neither here nor there. I hope she's truly happier now. I'd be grateful if you could pass along my thanks to her as a survivor for allowing her story to become history. I hope it helps some people in their quest for strength and educates others in the hell that can await the mere opening of your eyes.

Who knew it was a sin just to breathe?

- **Fionnuala Cullen**
  Belfast, Northern Ireland.

"*Greg. What can I say! WHAT A HEARTFELT BOOK. I wanted to read it faster but couldn't find the time due to work commitments, but I read it every spare minute I had in between work. SO REAL. SO TRUE TO MANY LADIES OUT THERE - Maybe Men Too! I found it Truthful, Desperate, Soulful, Dramatic, Sad, Tearful and Heart-Rendering. MY EMOTIONS WERE ALL CHALLENGED!*

I wanted to find her and put my arms around her and tell her she is AMAZING and a SURVIVOR.

I loved it Greg – I'm even emotional writing these words to you - I do love how you write and I loved the front and back covers as well.

Thank you from the bottom of my heart for letting me read and review it and for writing her story and I know that many others will read it and associate themselves with it."

- **Catherine Hartley**
  Belfast, Northern Ireland.

"*Firstly, I feel honoured to have read your book. It was an emotional rollercoaster of a read. I was so angry that she didn't leave from the start and put herself through all that trauma. I used to have very strong feelings with regards to people putting up with someone else abusing them. Why where they so weak to let someone treat them so bad? After reading your book I am left with only one feeling and that is of empathy. I get it now. I couldn't believe the statistic regarding how many attempts it takes someone to leave. It's a wonderful, hard-hitting and brutality honest read. I commend you for sharing your talent."*

- **Donna Connolly**
  Belfast, Northern Ireland

"Hi Greg. Well what can I say? As much as it pains me this lady's story rings so true to my own life. I think that's why I wanted to read it in the first place, just to know she was strong enough to leave.

I have read it all today, only putting it down to boil the kettle. I felt the hairs on my neck rise more than once, I was gritting my teeth and silently shouting "get out" or "leave him".

A gripping story of how love can be betrayed by an individual who decides it's ok to abuse the very person they're meant to protect. Despite everything she suffered she dug deep and stands a strong independent woman who even though I have never met, I am exceptionally proud of!"

- **Trish Mulholland**
  Belfast, Northern Ireland.

"I just finished this in one sitting. I was horrified; I felt like screaming at my phone. I cringed at each awful word he called her. Greg has brought out this beautiful woman's bravery with every word. His story telling hooked me from the title of the book, as he has with all his stories. He made me feel this could easily be a work colleague, a friend or a family member. We simply don't know what goes on behind closed doors. #IAM. Thank you both of you."

- **Siobhan McCaffrey**
  Saskatchewan, Canada.

"Raw and truthful, Greg tells her life as an abused woman starkly, and without frills. A thought-provoking book as to how some men think they can treat women."

- **Eva Beaudoin**
  Winnipeg, Canada.

"I can hear her voice telling the story. Genuine, real, authentic truth telling. Totally captivated my full attention at the outset of reading her story! It's giving me the courage to write my own story with no more hold backs! There is a power released in giving VOICE to truth that combats all of our "Don't Talk" rules of keeping us silent."

- **Teresa Steele Lydon**
  United States of America.

At Least He Wasn't Hitting You...

To Pat and Sallie!
With love and best wishes,
until we meet again,
Be Safe!
La Zenia 2018!

At Least He Wasn't

Hitting You…

Copyright © 2018 by Greg McVicker

First published edition: August 28, 2018.

Front cover photo by Engin Akyurt (pixabay.com).

Back cover photo by Shibari (pixabay.com).

Cover design by Greg McVicker and Trevor Harper.

Copy Editor: Mark Rickerby.

Book layout by Greg McVicker.

All rights reserved.

No part of this publication may be reproduced in any form, or by any means, electronic or mechanical, including photocopying, recording, or any information browsing, storing, or retrieval system, without permission in writing from the publisher.

ISBN:

978-1-989053-09-6 (Softcover)

978-1-989053-10-2 (eBook)

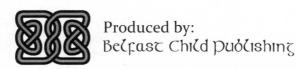

Produced by:
Belfast Child Publishing

At Least He Wasn't Hitting You...

A Personal Memoir

of

Abuse and Survival.

Written by Irish Author and Poet, Greg McVicker.

Table of Contents

At Least He Wasn't Hitting You...

*This story is dedicated to all those
women who have suffered silently
in their own abusive relationships.*

*This book is In Loving Memory
of those who never made it out alive ...*

"In life, we all have a cross to bear and a very unique story to tell; we just hope that someone will take the time to listen."

~ Greg McVicker.

At Least He Wasn't Hitting You...

A Personal Reflection from the Author.

"There's no greater agony than bearing an untold story within you."

- **Maya Angelou**

On the second day of writing this story for my dear friend whose identity will remain under a protective veil, it struck me like an electric shock that her experiences are similar yet different to that of another beautiful friend I know. Sadly, I have not seen that friend for many years now due to the bitter circumstances she herself is trapped within. Yet, despite the countless times I tried to council her and offered help, she always felt that if she did indeed seek help or take up my advice, she would end up dead.

I recently tried to find her to make sure that is indeed not the case. Regrettably, I was not successful in my efforts. I am hoping one day she reaches out to me and says she is okay, or that she finally found the strength and deep courage needed for her to leave behind the awful environment she has been trapped in for at least twenty-five years, perhaps longer.

If my memory serves me correctly, I wrote her story in 2008 and last saw her a few years thereafter. I am not sure if she has ever seen it, but she does know I went on to become an author. My main concern is to not traumatize her further, knowing the brutality of what she has endured and continually suffers is out there for others to read and relate to. On the contrary, I hope she would find comfort and redemption in the fact that she is not alone in her journey of grief and suffering. The traumas she has been exposed to go beyond human comprehension, often involving physical, mental, emotional and verbal abuse but, most of all, extreme levels of sexual violence.

I told her story in my first book, a personal memoir titled *Through the Eyes of a Belfast Child: Life. Personal Reflections. Poems.* It is an agonizing read and countless people have openly expressed their feelings about what she has endured and continues to endure at the hands of her predator. To protect her identity, using my social work training, I was extremely careful to not use any identifiers as to who she is, where she lives, or any other pertinent information. She is *one* face in the crowd, displayed beautifully for the outside world to view yet covered up with heavy make-up to hide the scars. She silently cries each night for what is expected of her if any man looks in her direction: anal rape.

My wonderful friend who asked me to write this book on her behalf spent countless hours recalling her experiences over the phone with me, with frequent check-ins to ensure she was okay while the book took shape.

I felt it is fitting to share a story titled *Bruised and Battered,* which I wrote twenty years ago for the other friend mentioned previously who survived horrific abuse. You will find this story followed by a poem of the same name. *Her perspective* is written in *italics,* and his perspective is in **bold print.** One is soft, loving, nurturing and gentle, while the other . . . well, just wait and see. I will let your emotions speak for themselves.

Greg McVicker, BSW.
Irish Author, Poet, Storyteller.

At Least He Wasn't Hitting You...

Introduction

"I walked a thousand miles just to slip this skin."

- **Bruce Springsteen**

If you are reading this book because you are in an abusive relationship, I hope you will come to see that my story *is* your story, my pain *is* your pain, and my grief and suffering most likely mirrors yours. However, I must let you know my experience is mine, just as yours is to you. We can all have similar life events but how we choose (or not choose) to work through them is what defines our inner strength and determination to not only save ourselves but to hopefully raise awareness and make change in the lives of others. Sometimes, we are not as fortunate in escaping from the bitter and brutal confines we find ourselves in.

I am purposely not sharing my name or my identity. If you are wondering why, it is because I want you to understand I am not just *one* woman who has experienced patterns of abuse, I'm simply *one amongst millions of women* who have crossed this harsh terrain but never asked for vicious or slanderous slurs to be cast against me by a man who swore before God to love, honor and cherish me.

I have carried these secrets around within me for twenty to thirty years; half my lifetime. I finally found the courage to share my story. Although I managed to get out of my situation alive, the cumbersome personal pain and internal suffering I carried on my shoulders all these grueling years is finally starting to be lifted. This will not occur overnight or through the publishing of this book. I won't kid myself. But if this helps others dig deep within and extract the courage and strength they themselves need to see light at the end of the tunnel, or the encouragement to seek help and make change before it is too late, then that is also healing for me. We are all born into this world with only one life to live. It should not be up to another selfish individual to dictate to us who *we* are, nor should we alter our characters and live our lives based upon how *we* are viewed in *their* eyes.

At Least He Wasn't Hitting You...

Please tell friends about this book; spread awareness that there is hope! I know there are others like me who have suffered and continue to suffer. Yet, my steady flow of tears has since become cleansing to me. I am sure that yours will be, too.

If you have not already done so, please realize we are not alone in our journey nor are we in any way, shape or form deserving of what we were are or currently subjected to. No matter what mental games have been used to groom you to their standards and image of who you should be, which is exactly what happened in my situation, please realize that you did not ask for this. And along with every venomous strike verbally cast upon you with a forked tongue curling around each hate-filled word while preparing for their next strike, the poisonous sting of each successive strike slowly sinking into your veins and continually drawing life out of you, please know you did not ask for this. I didn't, either.

When I uttered the words "until death do us part", it never crossed my mind it would occur *before* the passing of either myself or my partner. However, the death of our relationship occurred because the one person I loved with every ounce of my heart and soul, who I believed I would spend the rest of my life with, instead decided to take control of me as he did with the controls in the cockpit of his aircraft - a mechanical process of choosing my destination whether I wanted to go there or not.

If there is one thing you take away from this, I ask you please do not let people lead you to believe you are not being abused simply because you weren't slapped with an open hand, or punched with a clenched fist, or had skin torn from your body with teeth, or ended up with a bloodied face, or were dragged around by your hair and had it pulled out of your scalp, or kicked repeatedly with blunt force. Abuse comes in many forms, including physical, mental, emotional, spiritual, verbal, financial, marital and sexual. The list does not end there.

Each form of abuse is prevalent within today's society whereas my experiences occurred between 1990 to 2000. Then again, perhaps it is that we are now more aware of events such as these because the spotlight has been more brightly shone upon them. However, the cold fact that my ex did not lift his hand or fist to me provided fodder for many individuals, including my immediate family, to inform me that I was not an abused woman.

They were wrong then and they're wrong now. What the hell do they know about what I was experiencing since they were never in the same room with me in each instance that my torment was occurring? It is much easier to stand on the outside, looking in and making statements that have zero merit than to be in the same location while things are unfolding.

I am not an argumentative person. I accept the opinions of loved ones and acquaintances how they see fit. However, where I do draw the line is when they cast judgments against me with respect to my lived experienced. Had they walked in my footsteps or sat in my skin, night after night, wishing it would end or that I could find some way to escape, then they might have a different outlook on things.

As I have just told Greg who is writing this book for me, bruises heal as do broken bones. But, unfortunately, what has not healed is the damage done to my trust of everyone around me with the exception of very few people. There are times when I don't even trust myself; I guess that's part of the process of trying to figure out what the hell happened and how things got to where they were.

Nowadays, I find myself to be very suspicious of people and feel I am extremely damaged. I was not like this when I first entered the relationship with my ex. It has taken me years to deprogram myself and learn I cannot worry about what others think of me if they do not know my story. Yet I often ponder how many more out there have found themselves in the same predicament as myself.

To try and help push this further into the much-needed spotlight, and just like the

#MeToo movement which has been successful in calling out violence against women and bringing it into the forefront of peoples' minds, Greg is helping to create our own awareness movement by way of this book for both women and men alike. He has called it **#IAM**.

#IAM a woman and proud to be so regardless of the callousness of the names which have been cast against me countless times.

#IAM a loving daughter of another woman who gave birth to me yet did not expect me to have severe suffering inflicted upon me within the supposed sanctity of marriage.

#IAM the confidant to my cherished sister, one who I have spent several hours listening to on what she herself has experienced. However, when I tired to tell her what I was experiencing all those years ago when it was safe to do so, she refused to listen. She is the same way now. Nothing has changed.

#IAM a friend to many others who are unaware of my experiences, but this does not lessen them by any sense of the imagination. When scars are visible, people tend to ask how they were obtained. It is different when scars are invisible. The damage is within.

#IAM no longer afraid to say I am a survivor of marital abuse.

In saying all of this, I'm going to share specific and very traumatic stories. I am hoping these will unfold in a chronological format but to be quite honest, they probably won't. Right now, my focus is to put all my thoughts forward and to then pull it all together so that it hopefully makes sense.

The difficult thing with this, though, is that abuse never makes sense. I didn't ask for or sign up for it. I didn't do anything to earn it other than to become more compliant with each strike of his vicious and venomous words, including his words which sliced me to shreds like the sword of a samurai. Yet my experience has become my cross to bear.

My story does not apply to a person who comes from a 'lower socioeconomic status which is often seen as being "out in the open." Both visible and invisible abuse occurs. Visible is on streets, in public places and, tragically, often attached to those living in an impoverished condition that is not their fault. The "lower status" can occur in part as a result of class, race, gender, cultural beliefs and practices, political status or religious affiliation, as well as circumstances from which people are trying to climb out of and rebuild their lives.

Abuse is not limited to any particular race, class or gender, nor is it cured by any cultural belief or practice, political or religious affiliation, or geographic location. No one is immune. We are all victims of it at some point in our lives whether we recognize it or crumble to the belief that "*he*" or "*she*" wouldn't do that to you. They do. And in my case, ***he*** did.

I do not mean to sound conceited, but none of those socially constructed ideologies apply to me. My abuse was invisible - behind closed doors for the most part, but there were instances when it was exposed fully in public forums and settings. However, in those instances, not one person chose to step in and assist me. They all became bystanders. If this had occurred in today's world, with the mentality of society being what it is, bystanders would have pulled out their cell phones and recorded the confrontation for their social media accounts, hoping it would go viral and get them more likes and subscribers, caring not a bit about how its publication and the condemnations in the comments would further traumatize the victim. It is extremely sad what many communities have become. The advent of social media has not helped victims get the assistance they need when the abuse is actually occurring because everyone is too busy filming it.

As I was saying, I was in a different socioeconomic status. Not that we were self-made millionaires but my former husband was well-off financially. I, too, was in a very sound and secure job. Money was nothing to us. We had disposable incomes, the fancy house with a white picket fence, lived in the best

At Least He Wasn't Hitting You...

neighborhoods, drove the coolest cars and our circle of friends was from of an elite class compared to most. Yet none of this mattered. Contrary to popular belief, money did not buy happiness. It brought only misery. Lo and behold, I happened to be its chosen company. What mattered was how the hell I was going to get out of a toxic, damning relationship. Looking back now, I am convinced I was married to a sociopath.

As you read, please feel free to cry or laugh along with my story. If you want to feel angry, that is fine for I felt it. If you feel sad, then you too are experiencing my emotions of deep sadness. Perhaps if your feeling is that of being numb, then you have either already walked this path or are still in it and trying to figure out what your next move might be. As you will come to see, I have been there, as have many other women. Not by choice, either.

From the social work lens, Greg will tell you people may have lived similar experiences, but that each person processes it differently. It does not remove from you what you have gone through, as it does not me. Also know we are not alone and will likely find similar patterns in what we have experienced, especially those who are bewildered in that they are still breathing and managed to make it through that part of their past, regardless of being repeatedly told,

"At least he isn't hitting you..."

Greg and I would like to ask one small request of you as the reader – please add the hashtag **#IAM** to your social media posts. Please help us grow this awareness together. Our combined voices will speak volumes in drowning out abuse in its ugliest forms including mental, emotional, physical, spiritual, verbal, financial, and sexual.

Abuse is an unacceptable cancer. Let's put an end to it by creating a global campaign!

With my love to you all,

The voice behind this story.

Chapter One:

A Little Bit About Me.

"The journey of a thousand miles begins with a single step."

-   **Chinese proverb**

As you are already aware from my introduction, I will not be revealing my name. Just know that I am someone who is probably much like yourself. I grew up as a middle child of six, in a middle class, all-American Midwest family. I guess you could say there were a lot of "mid's", the biggest one being my marriage, which might be described as a mid-life crisis, though it occurred when I was twenty-eight.

I grew up in a nuclear family and was surrounded by good role models. I had never experienced abuse. My parents were together for almost fifty-five years until my father passed away, but not once did they lift their hands to their children. I knew from having a first-hand account of the longevity of my parents' marriage, that a home consisted of a couple who loved one another, had children, and raised them with wholesome values.

I went to elementary school before going on to become a freshman in my first year of high school. I worked my way through my course of study and graduated. I am quite competitive by nature and although I enjoyed participating in athletics and sports, I also loved writing and it came very easy to me. There was nothing out of the ordinary about my schooling. As both of my parents are in the field of education, this was a critical foundation in our family and was also very important to me.

At age eighteen, I went off to college and completed my degree within a four-year time frame. Although I fought with my siblings growing up, the thought of abuse never crossed my mind other than what I had heard about it through core classes I took at the beginning of my university studies.

By age twenty-two, I left university after having completed a post-secondary Bachelor of

Science undergrad degree in Education. From there, I began pursuing one job after another in teaching, all the while living what I believed to be a normal, charmed life. There was nothing out of the ordinary – I was following the same path I had learned from my parents.

My teaching career began at the elementary level for six years before thoughts of marriage had even crossed my mind. I was twenty-seven when I met who at first appeared to be the man of my dreams. I would later learn he was a false prophet would gradually begin his deconstruction of my inner being and every aspect of my life as I once knew it.

When we first began dating, the relationship was incredible. There I was with no children, never married, with a college degree, feeling like he rocked my world in every which way. At thirty-one, he was slightly older than me. He felt like everything was perfect and we were made for each other. Although, hindsight being twenty-twenty as it is, we probably pushed things too soon, and too fast.

I had briefly met him one evening two years prior when a friend introduced us to each other, but we were both speaking to other people that night and did not spend any sort of quality time with one another. I never saw him again until June of 1990.

We started dating that same month. By August of 1990, we were engaged. He was a charming fellow and showed the best side of himself, as people do when first getting together and learning about one another. I loved everything about him and did not see the early signs that things were going to go into a straight nosedive like a plane with engine failure. That's actually a very accurate way to describe the entire relationship, because he was a commercial airline pilot.

My suggestion was that we live together to get to know one another since we had only dated for two months. He was in complete disagreement with this. He argued that his mother would not be pleased with the arrangement. So I went along with his suggestion to make him happy and for his family's sake.

Within two months of dating we became engaged – one year later, we were married. As I had learned in my nuclear family, when you commit your life to someone, you see it through. Divorce was not an option. This was the first mistake I made but did not realize his intent or course of action. I guess it was the honeymoon phase, prior to us even being married. I was not from a broken home, nor did I follow a path of self-destruction. I came from a healthy family.

Chapter Two:

"You Are Nothing Without Me."

"The biggest coward is a man who awakens a woman's love with no intention of loving her."

- **Bob Marley**

In my mind, I was the polar-opposite of anyone who could or would wind up entering into an unhealthy relationship. I grew up in a loving, supportive, stable home environment. I earned a college degree so I could support myself and make my way in life, and I was successful in doing so. What I learned in university was how socioeconomic statuses often defined the path people found themselves in. Never in my wildest dreams would I have imagined this would apply to me.

As I have shared with you already, my former husband was a pilot and flew passengers across the world for a major commercial airline. To this day, this remains his career. As I told my story to Greg, it crossed his mind how many times my former husband uttered the words:

"Good morning, Ladies and Gentlemen, this is your captain speaking."

His passengers were the fortunate ones who got to hear the more pleasant side of his voice. Not because he wanted to be pleasant, but because he was *paid* to be. There was no way around it.

The moment the wheels touched the ground, his post-flight clearances were completed, and he was granted time off to come home, his tone immediately changed. This either occurred while he was en route to our house or perhaps when his co-pilot was receptive and the plane controls were set to auto-pilot. He could not drink to excess on the job, but that was not the case when he came home. He certainly made up for it. Nightly. I am not talking about a measurement of the richest, smoothest scotch either on the rocks, in a cocktail, or as a shot. It continued right through until he hit the ass end of the bottle.

He was hell bent on drowning out the demons in his tortured mind. And rather than being met with the pleasant words he would use during each flight with his passengers and cabin crew, I would instead be met with,

"You fucking cunt."

This charming phrase became a staple of the conversation when he got home, that was as soon as he walked through the door and put his bags down. There was no love, no kisses, hugs, or feverish pent-up sexual interludes upon his arrival. For me, it was a fear that became so instilled in me, I counted the very seconds until he took his bags out the front door and onto his next scheduled flight, where he would dish out his airlines pleasantries once again. Welcome to the friendly skies. Welcome to my hell.

It wasn't always this way. Actually, I do not know when it all began but I do know it took years for me to become that person who I still struggle to relate to. Many will wonder throughout this book why I stuck around for any of it, why I didn't walk out the door the first time he used that disgusting word. I still struggle with that question, too, and will do my best to answer it as we go along. For now, suffice to say catastrophes don't always happen all at once. Sometimes they happen a little bit at a time, so slowly and insidiously that you suddenly realize you have become someone you never thought you'd be.

During the process of becoming numb, life slowly ebbs away from you. From speaking with Greg, I now understand this is how the abusers work. They groom you to a point until you finally wake up one morning and do not recognize yourself in the mirror. Your sense of self is eroded. Everything you loved is no longer there. It certainly wasn't for me, including the person I once was. She, too, was gone.

The one saving grace I have right now, if it can be said, is that I did not totally lose myself. Perhaps a tiny part of my inner being recoiled into my body like a turtle does into its shell and stayed protected until it was safe to come back out. I kept hoping things would change.

Every day I prayed things would be different, for the betterment of not just me but my marriage. They didn't. They became worse.

At every opportunity, I was reminded by him, *"You are nothing without me."* That was coupled with his verbal flattery of telling me:

> *"You fucking dumb bitch. Women are useless! There is only one way to describe each and every one of them. Can't Understand Normal Thinking!"*

Sound familiar?

He always said those last four words in expressive tones through gritted teeth as if to underscore his statements and secure his thoughts about me.

Chapter Three:

"At Least He Isn't Hitting You."

"Some scars don't hurt. Some scars are numb. Some scars rid you of the capacity to feel anything ever again."

- **Joyce Rachelle**

I got married in June of 1991. Sadly, only three months into my marriage I knew that it was over and had to end. I had to get out. My first inclination to leave was when he called me a cunt for the very first time. I knew at that moment something was seriously wrong. At twenty-eight years of age, I was happily married. By Labor Day of the same year, I was in for the fight of my life.

The day after I first heard that word, he was playing in a golf tournament. He was a very good golfer and actually went on to win the tournament. Since I had undergone his alcohol-fueled tirade the night before, I did not want to go. My mind and stomach were not feeling up to it. He did not appreciate my absence, to say the least. Here he was being celebrated as a golfer who had just pocketed a big win and his wife was not on his arm, coddling up to him, playing the submissive spouse, and showering him with loving affection on his achievement. This did not go unnoticed by him, as the phone rang shortly after the fanfare died down with him screaming at me, using the same terms of endearment.

"You fucking cunt. You fucking bitch. Where the fuck are you? You're supposed to be here on my arm right now. How dare you humiliate me."

I simply replied I was not feeling up to it. Again, I reminded myself I needed to get out of this hell that I unexpectedly entered when I walked down the aisle three months earlier.

Five months into the marriage, I experienced an episode of even more horrific, vicious verbal abuse that convinced me I had to get out. He used to live in Colorado. We went out with his father to watch a Broncos football game. We

At Least He Wasn't Hitting You...

went to a bar to park our vehicle and then rode a bus to Mile High Stadium.

There was a chill in the air as we were walking out of the stadium so I walked at a brisk pace. He always walked at a slower pace, with his father walking behind him. As I reached the bus, I turned around, surrounded by crowds of people also waiting to board their buses, only to be met with him screaming at me.

"You stupid, fucking pathetic bitch. Where is my father? Christ. You walked far too fast and never went to check on him."

I hadn't walked with his father because I assumed he was, as he usually did. Within a few minutes of my arrival, with him still yelling at me in front of dozens of shocked people, his father showed up at the bus in perfect condition and confused about why his son was so upset. My stomach was churning, again thinking I had to leave my marriage. Not only was I humiliated by the man who I gave my hand and heart to in holy matrimony, it was done in front of a large audience of revelers coming out of an NFL football game.

I told my father-in-law I needed to leave. He knew his son was abusive but told me to not talk like that. Saving face for his son was more important to him than it was for his daughter-in-law to be safe in the sanctity of marriage. There was no safety or refuge to be found. The people who knew my husband's behavior always defended him. For the people who were unaware of his behavior, however, it was extremely embarrassing to be in the direct path of his verbal assaults.

His family members were well aware of what he was capable of but it was easier for them to recoil in shock or remain quiet rather than to speak up and confront him. I was teaching and did not want my colleagues to know what I was going through. My support system broke down extremely fast because his mother and father were big players in the church and often went out of pocket to help out with every cause. Who would believe me?

I had found one supportive person in the church but even that broke down quickly because I did not feel safe talking to him about the whole situation. Not now, but at the time. Because of the stigma surrounding this, I had trouble expressing what I was going through to even my closest friend, especially after she said:

"It is not life threatening when someone is screaming at you. At least he isn't hitting you."

Chapter Four:

Don't Chew, Just Swallow.

"A healthy relationship will never require you to sacrifice your friends, your dreams, or your dignity."

- **Mandy Hale**

I was always walking on eggshells. I started taking a lot of naps throughout the day because I was so mentally exhausted, I needed forty winks to escape from my reality. It was always a short reprieve from the nightmare I felt trapped in.

I didn't even realize at the time that my frequent napping was a result of depression. I was keeping the full extent of it under wraps, even from myself. It was never easy for me to pull myself together for dinner parties, which my husband loved to do. Actually, it was more of a chore.

When he was home from work, he would start with his name calling and fault finding, regardless of who the company was or where we lived. He always wanted to have the floor and all the attention centered around him. If the spotlight ever shifted away from him, there was hell to pay, but it was not always after our company had left. Sometimes it was during the visit and before dinner had even started.

By this time, we were living in Texas. These sudden gatherings, often unannounced with zero pre-planning, would occur after he had gone out to play a game of golf. He loved to make himself look larger than life and show off his goods. This did not entail a fake smile or a look of love from him to me as his partner, either. His eyes were dark brown, almost black to the point that they could have been made from the soul of the devil himself. Personally, I find brown eyes to be an attractive feature on any man. But over time, I began to see pure evil and hatred in the eyes I had once found so endearing; evil and hatred directed squarely at me. The saying, "If looks could kill" often came to my mind. Although it has been said the eyes are the windows to one's soul, in this case it was an open invitation to look straight into the depths of hell.

During one particular dinner party, his golf partner didn't want to hear from him as he had heard his stories far too often. For once, he asked to hear what *I* had to say, as I was never really allowed to speak while in the company of others. I was shocked at this and was not sure if I should respond or not. On one hand, I did not want to come across as being ignorant. But on the other, I knew my place. I also knew if I stepped out of line, I would not hear the end of it. I was damned either way.

This fellow asked me something, but before I could answer, my husband demanded all attention be placed back upon him. This was *his* show, *he* was the host, and how dare anyone challenge *his* authority in *his* own castle.

Dinner parties were frightening events as I was constantly on edge and didn't know what was going to happen. There was no relaxation or allowing things to unfold naturally. Anytime

At Least He Wasn't Hitting You...

I received a compliment about my appearance or how I kept my house, it was immediately deflected away from me by him. I couldn't even enjoy a simple word of praise because, through my forced smile, my mind had already burst into overdrive, an internal panic festering inside of me, knowing it would wind him up into a rage of jealousy. I would end up on the receiving end of his anger after our company left, or while they were still there.

On this particular night, dinner had been laid upon the table, but I had forgotten to place the butter dish. My husband's response to this was to scream at me, as I had ruined the perfect gathering of *his* friends coming to join *us*.

In his unhealthy mind, he thought they weren't getting the attention they deserved. They were attending a feast with His Royal Highness, or a wealthy prince or oil baron from the Middle East. My husband had delusions of grandeur in his imaginings of who he was to the circles of friends he kept, as if they were his pawns and I was his servant.

As he went into yet another violent rage, I finally hit a point of no return. Where this came from I do not know but unfiltered words which had never been uttered from my mouth suddenly erupted like a volcano which had been brewing beneath the earth's crust. Yet they came out slowly, were pronounced eloquently, and with deliberate delivery. I was horrified at what I was I hearing myself say but there was no stopping the flow. Regardless of what my heart was telling me, my mind said that I had to try and make my stand once and for all.

"Why don't you just shut your fucking mouth already and let the rest of us enjoy our dinner."

On another occasion, a childhood friend was in town visiting and came to see us with her husband. A glamour shot I had done for my ex that was in our living room caught the eye of her husband and he complimented me on it. My ex grumbled and said *he* paid for the picture even though I had arranged and paid for it myself and had given it to him for his birthday. Instead of accepting or appreciating

At Least He Wasn't Hitting You...

it, he saw it as wasted money and never saw anything in it, nor did he appreciate the lengths I had gone to get it done for him. Again, he found a way to contradict or diminish a compliment given to me.

The more he drank, the worse things got for me. One person said he thought I was really nice. My ex panicked and started saying everyone liked his wife more than him. I was amazed how a grown man with a professional career could act like such a child.

His ego always preceded his career; he needed it fed constantly. As much as he loved having a prestige status associated to being a commercial airline pilot, his concern about how his image was portrayed out of uniform took precedence. Someone with lower self-esteem would struggle, but I managed to make it through each day. But there was no victory, only more battle scars not visible to the naked eye.

Everyone who came to our home was from his circle of friends but never my own. Of those who did come over for a dinner party or to watch a football game, they did not hang around for long. We would see them socially for about a month or two, only for the friendship to either slowly fade away or abruptly end since he had an aura around him which inevitably revealed his true self. The men would quietly tolerate it, but their wives or partners wanted to get out of our house almost as quick as they had arrived. I am sure the drive home for many of our dinner guests must have been a real treat.

The only time I had any of my friends over was after he had packed his bags and went out for his next flight. It was a rare treat to share an evening with friends even though I was beyond mentally, emotionally, and physically exhausted. My husband never once said I couldn't do so, but I never told him about my little get-togethers because I knew he would grill me about everything I told them. It was easier for me to hide, and easier to chew on my own thoughts and swallow my pride to survive than it was to talk to him about this or anything else. To test this otherwise, I too may have ended up getting choked. Or worse, I

At Least He Wasn't Hitting You...

might have become one of those defenseless victims whose voices were silenced before their story could be told . . .

Chapter Five:

The Piranha versus The Goldfish.

"I didn't always know what I wanted to do, but I always knew the kind of woman I wanted to be."

- **Diane von Furstenberg**

Anytime I had to run to the store to do something or pick up a few items for our house, I would get ritually interrogated. The line of questioning began when I was getting ready in which I would first go to the bathroom to brush my hair or my teeth, or to put on some makeup to try and make myself look presentable to the public eye. This included me changing my clothes into something more decent before going out. Although I was trying to make myself feel better, to his mind, there was no way I could have possibly been doing this just for me. He suspected I was trying to be attractive for every man who looked in my general direction. How dare I!

At Least He Wasn't Hitting You...

His paranoia was excruciating. He refused to believe I was doing as I had told him and thought I was going to "fool around on him."

His paranoia eventually created paranoia within me, too. My happy self, the agreeable person I once was, began fearing what he was going to say or do when I went out and when I came home, when he would continue ripping into me about my time in the community, away from his side, and control.

I stopped trusting that he would just be decent to me or leave me alone As the marriage went on, he continued to wear and tear me down to the point that so much damage was done, I didn't know whether to tear it all down and start again or keep trying. My parents raised and provided us with an understanding of many wonderful family values, including the institution of marriage. It was perhaps for that reason that I hung in there.

It was 1993, two years later, when I realized I had checked out of my marriage. There was nothing left for me to fight for other than my own survival. The damage was irreparable. Although I was still physically in the marital home, I had become merely a shell of myself and was just walking around the house, existing, surviving, in a mindless, zombie-like state. It was frightening what I had become.

One day, as I wandered around, lost in my own thoughts, a memory returned to me . . .

I was in college visiting friends in a male dorm room and saw one of them had a piranha in his tank along with a goldfish. I noticed the goldfish had little chunks taken out of its tail.

I visited the same friends a few weeks later and saw that more bites had been taken out of the goldfish, its tail almost completely shredded. It was struggling to swim and stay away from the piranha but it had nowhere else to go.

As short time later, I returned to see the piranha finally had enough playing around in establishing its dominance and territory with the goldfish in his tank. Without warning, a full-scale attack occurred and the piranha shredded the goldfish to pieces.

Thinking back on that poor, beleaguered goldfish, I realized how much I had in common with it. I was being slowly devoured, too, but by words every bit as razor sharp as a piranha's teeth, and just as damaging. The body appears intact but the soul is in shreds. I also wondered if there would come a time when he would grow tired of toying with me and finish me off, too, like the piranha had done to the defenseless goldfish. The physical violence I witnessed that day had managed to escape my marriage, but the verbal assaults remained. My husband even repeated the words of my best friend on more than one occasion, as if I should feel fortunate . . .

"At least I'm not hitting you."

Once I saw the parallel between the goldfish and myself, it never left me. The tank was our home. I would walk around it only to be met with my husband's terms of endearment. Just like the piranha, he took pleasure in taking bites out of my raw flesh one chunk at a time with every vicious remark he cast in my direction. I fought to survive but had nowhere to go. I was not ripped to shreds in a physical sense but every other emotion and state of being was open game.

To be completely honest, that was one of the more pleasant stories I have to tell.

Chapter Six:

Pregnancies and Miscarriages.

"Maybe we feel empty because we leave pieces of ourselves in everything we used to love."

- **R. M. Drake**

During the marriage, I had one confirmed pregnancy and highly suspect I had more. The first two ended in the very early stages without any medical procedures having been done. The third one ended with the fetus dying within me at the three-month mark, as confirmed by my gynecologist.

Things had not been progressing well with the pregnancy. As I went on to learn during the ultrasound, it was discovered the fetus would not self-abort. I had to have a dilated and curettage procedure, also called a D&C. We went to a different doctor who was out of town by about an hour. However, right when I was scheduled for the procedure, which was sixty minutes before I was due to leave our house, my husband decided instead to leave for work so he could join his crew and catch their next flight together. He didn't even say goodbye to me that morning or offer any words of comfort and support. It would have been met with *"Fuck you"* or cold silence if I asked for a hug before he left.

In the days prior to undergoing this invasive procedure and during the long journey to the hospital, I quietly hoped he would be there waiting for me just so we could grieve this loss together as husband and wife, but he was nowhere to be found. Conspicuously absent, as the expression goes. It was my father in-law who took the time to bring me to the hospital. He was gentle and caring, whereas my husband was callous and cold towards me upon hearing the news of what had to happen. This was a complete about-face to his reaction when he first learned we were expecting.

My father in-law remained kind to me throughout this whole process and took me to dinner afterwards. It was only after we ate, as I

At Least He Wasn't Hitting You...

was reviewing the literature I was supposed to take home for my caregiver to review, that I realized I should not have eaten anything. One side-effect of anesthesia and such trauma to their body is nausea. I survived this, too.

I continued to endure the sleepy influence of sedation from the prescribed narcotics due to the agony I was suffering from the devastation to my uterus due to the removal of our unborn child. Because the fetus did not make it past the three-month stage, in some circles it would not be considered a human being. But for me, this *was* life. This *was* the gift bestowed upon me by the Creator in that it *was* my duty to produce offspring, to *have* a child, to *be* a mother, to *watch* her or him grow, and to *love and nurture* that infant when they made their presence known in this world. It was not to be. Just like the promises made at the altar, however, this too was not to be.

Two days after I had undergone the D&C, my husband expected me to do a huge favor for him. He was fully aware that I was still heavily medicated and in no position to drive by myself, especially for two hours to the airport but it made no difference to him whatsoever. He demanded I pick him up upon his arrival. And even though my body continued to wither in gut-wrenching agony, my so-called husband still couldn't find it in himself to express even the slightest bit of heartfelt sympathy for me.

Nil. Zilch. Nothing!

This provided me with my best insight yet into how insensitive he truly was. He was a cold-hearted bastard who took my hand at the altar and made all sorts of promises about in sickness and in health, then did nothing to help me in my time of need. All he did was complain.

Not long after the procedure was finished he was home and in one of his foul moods. As usual, he had been drinking and had to come up with additional ammunition to use against me. Since I was still healing, I didn't have the strength or the wit to stand up to him. He blamed me for the baby that had died inside my womb. He blurted out, "Because *we* are assholes, *we* do not deserve to have children." This led me to ask why I was being crucified for his bastard tendencies.

Such a sweetheart he was.

From 1991 to 1996, I gradually accepted the fact that my marriage was not going to get off the ground, so I started guarding my ovaries. What I mean by this is I only had sex two or three times a year with my husband. I rarely allowed him to touch me because we never had a connection. I ended up despising him since he showed me what our marriage meant and didn't mean to him. As I am a teacher and have seen plenty of kids in broken homes, not by choice, how could I consciously allow myself to get pregnant again knowing the kind of atmosphere that would be awaiting an innocent life. I knew I would have an uphill battle ahead of me in trying to get out of the marriage and as far away from him as possible.

In 1996, my husband got polluted as usual. He hid behind a glass of liquid piss this time to gain the courage required to bring up trying once again to have a baby. As he had worn me down more times than not with the promise that he was going to be an "okay person" and stop abusing me, I voluntarily took myself off of the pill in a last-ditch effort to save our relationship from complete destruction. I was blinded by love but even more desperate to not fail. We did get pregnant again and for two months or so, he struggled to suppress his abusive tendencies. But as with each time before, the baby died along with my hopes not only for new life, but for the magic only a baby can provide to save this nightmare of a marriage. And magic was what it needed. Lord knows I tried everything else.

Even after I had the D&C, we didn't use contraceptives. No condoms, no pills, no IUD. Perhaps because I fell into an undiagnosed state of Stockholm Syndrome, we tried again and again to have a baby. Another failed attempt occurred which, in hindsight, was a blessing in disguise.

In 1997, we left the Midwest and moved to Texas. I was torn about relocating. My limited support system would have its umbilical cord severed completely. I did not dare put myself in that predicament. But he convinced me I needed to go with him and that we should stay together because we were married and had to stick it out regardless of the turmoil. He told me things would be different and it was a new start for us since all the negative influences in his life would be removed.

By doing so, he made his gripe sound completely legitimate. He blamed *my* family and *his* family, especially *his* mother with whom he had a love/hate relationship since she spent much of her time antagonising him. They could not get along with or without each other. He promised that since his drinking buddies couldn't drag him off to the golf course, they wouldn't be able to influence our lives anymore. Promises, promises. This led me to go against my better judgment.

Because he was so convincing, I decided to give it a shot and actually felt he deserved yet another chance. I depended on his words of encouragement. Yet once again, they became compounded lies as his old ways and patterns soon returned.

Once there, he joined another country club. When he was off work and began making new friends, which of course was great for him, I learned they too were drinkers and that he had gone back to what he knew and did best – drink. It wasn't long before things broke down for me. My family was one thousand miles away and could not possibly know what was going on. Again I found myself back in hell's half acre.

I had to find a new teaching job. When I got hired in Texas, they had to get the contract figured out and what my rate of pay would be. However, the district members kept dragging their feet. I also had to get my transcripts sent in which took time to process. This was not good enough for my husband because he wanted to know what my income would be.

They called me a Yankee since I was from up north but I tried to put my best foot forward. Then my ex stepped in and started raising a ruckus. He phoned the principal at

At Least He Wasn't Hitting You...

the school I had applied to and called her out, demanding to know why I didn't have a job.

This was not done out of a desire to help me - it was for control, just like he wanted to control the direction of our marriage by bringing a child into what would have been a very toxic environment. It would not have been fair for the child to experience this. And as selfish as it might sound, it wouldn't have been fair for me, either.

From that point on, I remained off birth control pills and all other forms of contraception permanently because there was little to no sexual activity except for a one-off sometime within the year. My decision to never have babies with him was further solidified.

There would be no more pregnancies. No more miscarriages.

Chapter Seven:

The Republican versus The Democrat.

"I believe the root of all evil is abuse of power."

- **Patricia Cornwell**

We were aware of each other's differing political affiliations before we got married but it was not a deal breaker for either of us. We went on with life and did not let this get in the way. At least not until one day . . .

A Governor's election, also known as a gubernatorial race, was well underway. My parents taught me to exercise my voting rights. They were well-informed about current events, politics, and world news.

Even at a young age, I was curious about politics. In 1972, when I was nine years old, before the Watergate scandal came to light, I already had a dislike for President Richard Nixon. In my heart, I wanted him out of office and George McGovern, a Democrat from South Dakota, to be our President.

After elections, I asked my parents who they voted for. Always very tactful, they told me voting was part of their civic duty and, their right as American citizens, and they did not discuss it with their friends or anyone else for that matter.

I was making my way home from work and stopped to vote. I pulled up to a polling station and checked off my choice on the ballot sheet before depositing it into the ballot box. I voted the Democratic ticket as my husband knew I would. He was out golfing, which meant by that afternoon he had already consumed a large quantity of alcohol and was fired up discussing politics with his Republican buddies. In turn, this meant I was in for a huge screaming battle as soon as our paths crossed.

Sure enough, when he made his drunken entrance shortly after I arrived home, the first words out of his mouth were,

"Did you vote today?"

My answer to the question I knew he would ask was simple.

"Yes, I did."

I could tell by his stance and obviously drunken state that this was not going to be a pleasant exchange. He wasn't going to accept my basic answer, nor was he going to allow me to have the final word. Then came his unsolicited truth or dare question, as expected.

"Who did you vote for?"

I immediately responded with what had been ingrained in me by my parents.

"I don't feel the need to discuss it with you."

Once again, he asked me the same question, slowly spelling it out this time, pausing on each word with hatred glowing in his eyes.

"You had better listen very carefully to me. Who. Did. You. Vote. For?"

No matter how many times I stuck to my position of exercising my civic right as an American citizen, knowing he was doing his damn best to pick a fight, he continued his cruel grilling. It became progressively worse with each statement, with him demanding to know, all the while unleashing his venomous tongue with continued strikes, which were now beginning to be interjected with his favourite word choice to describe me. Although I tried to remain strong and stand up to him, he continually swatted my comments aside.

"Who did you vote for, bitch? Did you hear me? I already know that you voted. Now shut the fuck up and quit arguing with me. Who did you vote for, you fucking bitch? You are not leaving this kitchen until you tell me who the fuck you voted for. How can you be such a stupid, fucking dumb cunt in that you cannot answer a simple goddamn fucking all American question asked of you. You call yourself a teacher? Let me say this. You are nothing but the worst teacher I've ever known. In fact, you know what you are? A stupid, teaching bitch who is

nothing more than a cunt and does not know her place in society or under my roof invading my space!"

If felt as if his sadistic, acerbic words were slashing through raw flesh and solid bone. The blood rose to my face, my heart raced, and my pulse thumped so hard, it felt as if my jugular vein might burst and cover the fucker in my blood, which he probably would have enjoyed. I finally broke my silence.

"I voted for the democratic candidate! There's your answer! Is that what you wanted to hear? Satisfied?"

As if things had not already been in a state of nuclear crisis with the boiling point approaching at breakneck speeds with me as his target lock, stock and barrel, this was the chance he was waiting for to really pull out all the stops, drop the green flag and push both buttons together.

"Are you kidding me? Fuck you, who Can't Understand Normal Thinking! Did you hear me? FUCK YOU! How

At Least He Wasn't Hitting You...

*fucking dare you cast a vote for that
pig-headed, liberal-loving cunt!"*

As if his words hadn't already shredded
most of my inner being, he needed affirmation
that I indeed followed my political affiliation
and voted for the Democratic slip. It was an
informed choice. It was what my parents had
taught me to do. He couldn't stand not
knowing if I had gone with my instincts,
seeking change in the administration, as well
as our Commander-in-Chief who would lead
our country into the twenty-first century. As a
citizen it is my civic duty. It is my birthright.
The USA. We, the people . . .

It was also my right to keep it private, from
everyone, as my parents had always done.

He was ready for not just an argument or a
fight but an all-out onslaught which had been
stewing and brewing in his turbulent mind
throughout the day while he was out golfing
and drinking. As his screams unfolded second
by ear-splitting second, life for me went into a
brief lull and pause for thought. How is it, I
thought, that he can take his seat behind

instrument panels brimming with controls, lights, levers, buttons and pedals and fly the damn thing without going kamikaze, all the while knowing full well the three hundred people or so seated behind him come from various political beliefs and backgrounds? Did he ever consider making his announcements the way he spoke to me about their voting choices but using his airplane etiquette?

The scene began unfolding within my tortured mind:

"Ladies and Gentlemen, this is your Captain speaking. We are currently cruising at 38,000 feet. It's a long way down so you might want to listen to this announcement carefully. Before we land this aircraft, I want each one of you to tell me how you voted in today's gubernatorial race. I'm sure you followed the lead of your Captain and voted Republican. You made not only the right choice, but the only choice! For this, I will grant

At Least He Wasn't Hitting You...

mercy on your souls. Perhaps you will meet our next governor hopeful who I just happened to vote for. We are flying over The Cornhusker State which is where our former Commander-in-Chief, President Ford, was born. God Bless America.

We know you have options, so thank you for flying with us today on Antagonist Airlines - Where you do as we tell you to, or else!"

The thoughts in my mind had obviously become twisted in trying to find a way to prepare myself for what was coming next without really having a chance to breathe from his first attack. There was no challenging his beliefs, as he would argue until he was quite literally red in the face, all the while matching the color scheme of the Grand Old Party. Yet as if a fist met my jawline full on, my fleeting milliseconds of reprieve burst.

"What the fuck is wrong with you? Are you fucking stupid? What the fuck are you doing voting for

fucking liberals? What the fuck? Are you fucking kidding me? You stupid fucking cunt. I voted for the Republican ticket. Our two votes just cancelled each other out. Our friends did the exact same thing. All because of you they made that choice. You probably told them to do the same. This beautiful country is doomed because of you. FUCK! You deranged, pathetic cunt."

And that was that.

The uncontrollable rage had reached its own form of ejaculation as it spurted and spilled out of his mouth. He did not say sorry and refused to discuss it further.

I quickly learned to let things like this go. He would not acknowledge the event or the eruption of his pent-up anger and hatred, which was always unleashed onto my awaiting ears and defenseless mind, heart and soul. His buddies were never on the receiving end of his brutal, unfiltered rage. I was front and center for it every single time.

The Democrat won the election and defeated the Republican, but it did not end there. He and his equally Republican mother made every effort to throw it into my face that my vote had perhaps helped the Democratic party vote by cancelling their votes out, and I was forever the biggest fucker for doing so. I heard about it throughout our entire marriage, ever since the Clinton's were elected in 1992. They remained at the helm and, sure enough, steered the USA into the new millennium. This also happened to be during the vast majority of my marriage.

To say my husband took umbrage with the outcome of the election is to put it very mildly. He stopped at nothing, even going as far to say the USA was fucked. He continued his rants, along with his mother, at every waking moment, jabbing me about Democrats being in the Whitehouse, my liberal music and magazines, the liberal books I read, and my crazy, liberal viewpoints.

As if that wasn't enough, they blamed the collapse of my marriage on this.

Chapter Eight:

He Always Drove.

"A man's ego is just as fragile as a woman's heart."

- **Lana Del Rey**

I had offered many times throughout our marriage to drive our car, but my husband had an obsession - he had to be the one behind the driver's seat. In *all* aspects. The same can be said about his planes. *He* was the captain and he alone made the decisions for everyone else.

His sister and I were picking him up one day from the airport, which was about two hours away from where we lived. It was late at night when his flight returned so there wasn't much traffic.

I had gone along for the ride to keep her company. Since we did not get to see her very often, I felt this was a good time to get to know my sister-in-law a little better. I found the tone

At Least He Wasn't Hitting You...

of her conversation to be quite different than that of her younger brother. I could talk with her and not have to wait with baited breath for her to unleash some inner monster, ripping me to shreds in the process. Without question, I preferred this over his way.

We arrived at the airport and decided we didn't need to go inside to meet him because he could simply come through the terminal after going through his deplaning security clearances and meet us in front of the airport.

We had timed our arrival to perfection so we didn't have to wait long. Since his sister was there with me, the time passed much faster.

We were deep in conversation, talking about recent events in the news and chatting about things in general but there was no discussion about the troubles in our marriage. I didn't need him finding any more reasons to erupt like Mount St. Helens without a moment's notice.

He came out of the airport right on cue with his luggage. Seeing his sister and I standing there for him, one might of thought he would have kept his cool. He didn't.

Even the cold chill in the Nebraska air didn't seem to faze him. His sister and I sat in the same seats of the vehicle we had driven to the airport in, myself in the passenger seat and she in the driver's seat.

He made his way to the rear of the vehicle – a large SUV – and placed his belongings in the back. From there, he walked around to the driver's door and was getting ready to get in when his sister rolled the window down, looked at him and said, *"Get in the back."*

In an instant, he was ready for war. Any female who told him what to do would not go unpunished. His response was immediate. Once again, it did not hold any of the pleasantries he probably uttered forty-five minutes earlier while preparing to land or thanking his passengers.

"I'm driving. It's my vehicle. I pay for the gas. I pay for the insurance. And besides, I shouldn't have to explain myself. I always drive."

At Least He Wasn't Hitting You...

It was a loud, firm, forceful statement. However, I noticed a stark contrast between how he spoke to his sister and how he spoke to me. Most notably, he didn't call her a stupid, fucking bitch. He never once let a swear word leave his mouth. Nor was she told that women are all the same and *"Can't Understand Normal Thinking."* There was no venom in his choice of words. He was not ranting or raving, nor was he pressing her about making a stand. He was not controlling. Direct, but not derogative.

I sat for a moment wondering how it was he could suddenly present himself in this way, for I knew nothing of the sort. I had forgotten he could be so nice to someone, as it has been a very long time since I saw that side of him.

Our response was just as swift as his. His sister and I looked at each other and burst into fits of laughter at his stupidity. Here he was, growing mad like a child without a present on Christmas morning, sulking on the outside of his vehicle, posturing, and trying to make stupid demands of his older sister.

In the end, with the two of us still laughing, she finally relented and vacated the driver's seat. It was easier to do this than to challenge him. She knew what he was like and perhaps could not stand the thought of seeing her baby brother having a fit after a flight, looking like The Incredible Sulk in his pilot's uniform. It wasn't worth fighting over. She knew he would just rant and rave until he got his way. If that meant we would have all been left sitting in the cool Nebraska air at midnight until we gave in to his demands, he was prepared to do so.

Being his typical, ignorant self and not giving a damn about anyone else, he climbed into the cockpit of his SUV, lit up a cigarette and refused to open the window, leaving the two of us coughing and spluttering from the second-hand smoke he exhaled. He drove us mad while he drove us home!

His childish pride was satisfied, thinking he had succeeded in winning the driver's seat back, but all he really succeeded in was driving me further away from him.

At Least He Wasn't Hitting You...

Chapter Nine:

Past Due Payments.

"When you see crazy coming, cross the street."

- **Iyanla Van Zant**

My ex was notorious for paying bills late. He was so egotistical he believed he had the right to pay people when they were lucky enough to get money from him. However, if the shoe was on the other foot and money was owed to him, well, that that son of a bitch had better cough it up quick or there would be hell to pay.

Prior to the days of Caller ID, I received several calls from people demanding money from us. We were still living in the Midwest at this time. He would not let me pay for any of the bills, even though he was gone most of the time and we had the money available. It didn't make any sense to me. His standard response when asked about the bills was,

"Fuck them! I'll pay them when I feel like it!"

When he left the house to report for duty, he would drive to the nearest airport, which could be an hour or two away, and then fly out. He was based out of New Jersey and then Texas. Bills were of no concern to him, nor was he concerned about how I would be impacted if they weren't paid. He had a foolproof *"I can do whatever the fuck I want"* attitude as he came and went as he pleased.

He never had to worry about the electricity being turned off in the hotels he would sleep in, or the plane not having the bill paid for prior to the engines being fueled for departure. And even if he did, he probably would have told the ground crew to "do their fucking jobs" or they would be responsible for three-hundred crew members and passengers pissed off because they were not getting their needs met and were being saddled with delays, as well as the plane possibly falling out of the sky and bursting into a ball of flames.

On one occasion while he flew around the world, I couldn't wait to leave work and go

At Least He Wasn't Hitting You...

straight home to look after myself. Upon my arrival, I went through my usual routine of opening the garage door and then entering the house. However, on this night, I couldn't get the garage door to open or go up, nor could I lift the door manually. I thought perhaps the batteries had died in the remote control for the garage door. And since I never carried a key for the front door because I always entered through the garage, I was forced to call a locksmith. That too was embarrassing.

As soon as he unlocked the door, I could tell immediately that the electricity had been shut off. Since my husband was working, he didn't have to go through the inconvenience of contacting the electric company or paying them with a credit card to have the services restored. It was a hurtful and embarrassing situation that never should have happened in the first place. I was the recipient of all heat now placed upon me from the companies to whom we owed money, without rhyme or reason.

As if that weren't bad enough, one time my principal called me into his office. A feeling of dread swelled up in my throat as I thought to myself, "What could I have possibly done to be pulled into the office?" I felt like a student called in for a detention hearing.

I kept myself composed as best as I could only to be informed that as a teacher, someone instilling good family values into children with whom I was trusted by dozens of parents, my wages would be garnished. The madness of my husband saying "Fuck you!" to the companies who sought payment for the services they provided had now damaged my professional life, too. The craziest thing is we had money in the bank and could have had everything paid in advance and in full, and could have always been in a credit situation. The chaotic dysfunction of my husband's mind must have been placed on autopilot mode.

It was levied onto my shoulders to look after bills while he was away on his job and making his announcements of weather conditions and arrival times to his passengers, none of whom

At Least He Wasn't Hitting You...

knew he was an abusive, drunk husband and that his wife was left to struggle with debt collectors constantly calling while he flew the friendly skies.

Things got worse the day I came home to find a Corvette parked in our driveway. He stated bluntly that he could afford it, so why not? He was very materialistic and wanted to show his wealth while his pockets sat empty, as did the accounts of those we owed money to. Things went from bad to worse to beyond logical reasoning. Quite simply, it was a catastrophe!

I decided I needed to have an outlet from all the pent-up stress so I joined the YMCA. The monthly membership fee, which would be coming out of our joint checking account, was a measly $22.00 per month. Although we were members of an expensive country club and could afford that, but it was more for him to satisfy his desire to golf and show off his wealth. But he freaked out and condemned me for not asking *his* permission to have my cheap YMCA membership since the money was not being used to pay our bills. In his mind, it was a misappropriation of funds. How dare I do such a thing? To that, his stock statement always was:

> *"I have money and can afford it. I will do what I want! But YOU had better ask for MY permission before wasting MY money on unnecessary items, you useless fucking cunt!"*

Although I tried to engage him on the importance of paying utility bills to avoid debt collectors being sent after us, he saw this as me being trivial.

He spent a lot of time on the telephone with his mother and friends. Most of the time, it was his mother he called. He spent upwards of $250 per month on these phone calls yet was furious when I spent a little bit of money on myself as a release. He made damn sure I knew everyone else in his life was more important.

He made sure I was his verbal punching bag and unleashed a fury of vocal blows upon me, yet called others to have polite conversations

At Least He Wasn't Hitting You...

with them. Those were often saturated with statements of self-flattery about how wonderful he was. Yet to me he would say "Shut the fuck up, you bitch" if I tried to engage him. However, he went nuts whenever I used the *I* word . . .

"Here's what I think" or "I don't feel well."

Any statement with the word I in it was met with resistance and the accusation that I was only thinking of myself.

I was often told I was "fucking selfish." I wondered what I could say to help him engage with what I was feeling. Would it be better to start using "the royal we", such as "we are not happy, we are not well, or we need to go to the bathroom" just to satisfy his self-serving and nauseating arrogance.

Somewhere along the line he got it into his head that "no one knows how to play the game because the rules are constantly changing." I felt so helpless. I could not play the game to change the total control over me he insisted upon. Remember what he already thought about me and his description of almost every other woman he knew . . .

"Can't Understand Normal Thinking!"

When we got to Texas, he finally learned he needed to get his act together. We came to an agreement that I would take care of the mortgage and he would be responsible for all of the other bills. Thus, we agreed to split our checking accounts, maintain separate bank accounts, and monitor our own statements. Well, at least I did.

Separating our accounts may have been the impetus I needed for me to reach my final straw and get away from him. I started saving money, enough to protect me financially.

But even after all the trouble his refusal to pay bills on time had gotten us – correction, me – into, he still refused to see the importance of getting money into the hands of the service providers. Not only were my wages garnished for the other bills, there was an occasion where he had not covered my dental expenses, which ended up making what can only be described as headline news. The local paper had a public naming and shaming process in which they published the names of anyone owing money. You can imagine the misery of having my name in black and white print in the daily paper, telling the world and the local community about how we neglected to look after paying the simplest of household utilities.

My husband failed to understand that this was not just *his* money, it was *our* money. I was bringing home an income, and although it was nowhere near what he was making, I worked extremely hard for it. In his eyes, however, this made me inferior to him. There were several double standards going on, especially with the finances. Since our bills remained habitually paid late or not paid at all due to his irrational resentment toward utility companies simply wanting compensation for their services, my stress continued to grow along with our debt.

Chapter Ten:

Suicide Solution.

"There are many who don't wish to sleep for fear of nightmares. Sadly, there are many who don't wish to wake up for the same fear."

- **Richelle E. Goodrich**

I began to have thoughts of suicide. I can't even begin to tell you where or when this began or what sequence of events brought it on within the timeframe of our marriage. What I do know, however, is that we were still living in the Midwest during this time. No matter what I said, I could not get through to him to let him know how I felt. I was always fearful of how he was going to react or what he was going to say. Besides, I knew anything I said would be used against me.

During this time, I kept telling him I wanted to seek counselling to the point that I was finally begging him to go. The reason he didn't want to go is that he knew he was being a blatant, bitter asshole and that someone was going to tell him what he should or should not be doing, including his abusive ways. He told me that he was pretty much checked out as everything which was wrong with the marriage was *my* fault. If the dishwasher didn't work, it was *my* fault. If a door handle was broken, *I* was to blame. If there was no fuel in the vehicle, that too fell on *my* shoulders. He tried to validate his crazy thoughts by using the line:

"Anyone who wants to seek counselling is the one who has the problem."

He was non-cooperative, to say the least. Even though I could have and eventually did seek counselling by myself, he was not willing to go whatsoever. How dare anyone tell him he was wrong? In his mind, he could not park his pride and his ego to address the fact that his marriage was taking a nosedive into the toilet. Mentally, I was already there but I maintained the belief I was not ready to give up. I wanted to try to make things work and turn it around.

But then came the day when I completely checked out. Even though I was still in the marriage, I was a lifeless, cloned shell of myself in an even deeper, almost catatonic state. I did not recognize myself as being human anymore, a daughter, his partner, or, most of all, as a woman who needed love, touch, engagement, intimacy, her needs met, intimate conversations, a smile, or even a telephone call to see how I was doing while he was out flying around the world. These were completely absent. Everything a marriage should be made up of, including the raging hormonal desire for me to jump him as soon as he walked through the door, strip him of his uniform and ravish him as if there was no tomorrow, was graveyard dead. There were no feelings of affection from him, no hello, no kiss, no hug, not even an unanticipated, animalistic fuck in the middle of the night to expel pent-up sexual desires and leave the two of us collapsed in drenched exhaustion. Any fantasies I once had of having intense sexual engagements and mind-blowing orgasms with my husband had flat-lined long ago.

At Least He Wasn't Hitting You...

Suicide had crossed my mind in the past because of his abuse and feeling as if I were trapped, but self-destructive thoughts started to consume me. I believed I had no other choice but to end my life and put this torturous part of my life behind me once and for all. And today happened to be that day.

What I decided to do was to take a cocktail of pills that we had in the house. I didn't even know what they were. After I swallowed them, I walked into the kitchen and saw that my husband was there. There was nothing I could do other than collapse onto the floor in front of him as my legs buckled beneath me.

In the medical profession, they say hearing is the last thing to go during the end stage of life. As my heartbeat slammed against my eardrums, my head thumping and throbbing from my fall, I was not met with words of panic or by him frantically dialing for emergency medical personnel to come to my side and pump my stomach full of charcoal in order to empty it of its pharmaceutical contents. Instead, I heard him screaming at the top his lungs, then standing over me. In my state of overdose, I assumed he was uttering his usual loving words to me. A fucking bitch. A motherfucking waste of skin who was nothing but a useless cunt and couldn't teach anyone how to add let alone read the instructions of how to be a proper, perfect, and respectful wife. How dare I do something so drastic to waste his time?

He left me lying on the floor for a long time.

My recollection of this was taking the pills, collapsing, and lying on the floor in a semi-conscious state. I listened carefully yet there did not seem to be any signs of sirens ringing in my head or flashing lights with paramedics banging at the door, strangers speaking to me, asking my name, date of birth, blood type, or what I had taken. There was no beeping of equipment or heart monitors beside me, nurses running around frantically from the direction provided to them by the attending physicians. I was not sure if I was in emergency, purgatory, or dead. Every thought

At Least He Wasn't Hitting You...

which rattled around my head in trying to kickstart my brain was met with fog.

He hadn't even called for an ambulance, nor would he have cared to call the coroner if I was indeed dead. He was most likely checking our cabinet of files to see if he could find the insurance papers to add more money to our bank account, only to not pay the medical bills for having my lifeless body removed from the home. Instead, he would step over my corpse and leave me there to rot because picking it up would have taken far too much effort. I did, however, manage to drag my almost paralysed body up off the floor and onto my bed.

This was the only time I tried to kill myself. It was definitely a cry for help but did not get his attention whatsoever. It was not successful in taking me out, either. In hindsight, I think I tried this for him to hopefully see the extent of my pain and how much I hurt from the toxicity of our relationship.

If I had been successful, he most likely would have gone out for a game of golf before raising a toast to being finally free of his anchor. Other than being his proverbial cunt, he had no use for me. If this had happened on a plane with only one parachute and the two of us were onboard, I am sure he would have told me to jump first as he was trained in skydiving and would follow me out only to say that I fought him off and wanted him to save himself since so many passengers would be relying on him for his next flight, before receiving a medal of honor for the bravery of his actions.

I eventually did go out to meet with a counsellor who happened to be a pastor from a local church. When I described my situation to him, he told me my husband was not to blame for the words being spewed and spat in my face on a daily basis, but that it was only the alcohol speaking. Had the heavens opened up and struck me dead with a large bolt of heat-seeking lightning for the thoughts circulating within my mind, it would have been a welcomed relief.

As for my suicide solution, had it not failed, it would have been an easy way out for him. Better yet, it would have been easier for me.

When I look back at this episode which happened approximately twenty-five years ago, it scares me to think that my zombie-like nature was in that space that I actually thought this was a "solution." Suicide is always easier than life, of course. The finality and oblivion of death erases the need for hard decisions and the courage to follow through with them. But as the saying goes, it's a permanent solution to a temporary problem. If I had killed myself that day, I would never have known the joy I would ultimately achieve later in life, including sending this book into the world, which, though it may not seem so at this particular chapter, is a declaration of independence – and, yes, victory.

Chapter Eleven:
Evil Task Master.

"When a deep injury is done to us, we never heal until we forgive."

- **Nelson Mandela**

My husband often felt he needed to show me how to do things and took sick pleasure in giving me a lesson, knowing full well I was not able to perform the task to his exacting standards. I was unable to develop a habit quickly like he did. He relished in this fact, as it reinforced and displayed his power and control over me. He was the puppet master and I was his marionette.

He occasionally gave me a golf lesson. It was in his blood to do this to anyone whom he felt was beneath him. And although he himself had several faults, I refused to point them out to him as blatantly as he did mine. It would have led to another crucifixion during which a

At Least He Wasn't Hitting You...

crown of thorns from the carefully pruned rosebushes in our pristine garden would have ended up on my head.

I must say he was and remains an excellent golfer, but he severely lacked the patience required to teach someone, or at least me. Had he been a good teacher properly trained to give lessons, he would have known patience is part of the game. Then again, how could I possibly know what a good teacher was? He referred to me as being nothing more than a *"stupid cunt"* more times than I care to remember. He also felt that my university education, which I attained to better the lives of the children with whom I worked, made my students worse off, not better.

Along with the hairs on the back on my neck standing on edge when he taught me anything, I always cringed. The reason for this is that he would rapidly chuck insults at me when I could not develop his perfected habits and traits on command. He took great offense when I was unable to swing a golf club to his standards of improvement immediately after providing me his lesson, or at least within ten swings of it. He felt I should have developed the skill to do so immediately instead of wasting his time and energy. No matter how hard I tried or worked feverishly trying to improve myself in all aspects to be the best wife for him, my efforts were often in vain.

I clearly remember his verbal abuse on the driving range in front of others. His filter was non-existent; he didn't hold back as he went into one assault after another.

"Come on! You call yourself an athlete? You can't do something as simple as hit the ball straight down the fairway!"

He was relentless. His statements, peppered with a few choice words, were uttered ever so slightly under his breath but were heard by all. No matter what I did or tried to do, there was no way of pleasing him.

"I showed you a better way to play and you simply can't or won't do it."

Because I didn't operate or act like him, I perpetually found myself being wrong or, in his opinion, *"belligerent"*. Regardless of my repeated cries, begging and pleading him to leave me alone so I could practice what he instructed me to do, he continued to harass me.

In his eyes, I was never good enough, nor could I function at his level or personal standards. In his mind, he was a god amongst men, a legend, while I was some pathetic fuck whom he had taken pity on. In his ongoing attempts, he made it *his* mission to sculpt and improve my sense of self through *his* defined image of what *I* should be. Even when each stage of *his* personally-crafted ideology had been completed and perfected, it was impossible for me to maintain since he would find some fault in it which was mine to hang my head in shame for. How dare I not become what he wanted or expected me to be?

One time, we decided to go downhill skiing. Again, since he had been skiing since he was four years old, his skillsets were well-defined while he was out on the slopes. He had thirty years of honing and perfecting how he maneuvered both swiftly and with sleek turns as he effortlessly glided over the powdery fluff beneath him. He made it look so easy. I had skied only a handful of times before meeting him. And I was going to get a lesson from him whether I wanted it or not.

I was surprised he didn't tell the lift operator how to use the controls to ensure the ski lift was as smooth as silk as we were brought up the face of the mountain. Knowing how he bragged about each flight, how he could tackle the strongest crosswinds while bringing his passengers down and onto each runway without them even knowing they had landed because of his finesse and expertise, I expected much the same here.

"Take it slow, steady, easy. I want no bumps, no jerky movements, and you better make goddamn sure that we land just like I do on the wings of each eagle I fly. If you fuck this up, you will wish you had never met me in the first place. I will ensure they

At Least He Wasn't Hitting You...

fire your pathetic ass if you make a
mistake with me on this lift. Got it?"

We reached the top of the mountain only to
be immediately met with an extremely difficult
run. He loved to take this on and then show or
brag about how he could conquer it without
breaking a sweat. Every other skier, however,
was met with a challenging berm as soon as
they had exited the ski lift and headed
downhill. But no matter how hard I tried, I
couldn't get the hang of that cursed thing. Of
course, my unfettered husband stepped up to
the plate as he was solely determined to *"teach
his stupid cunt wife"* how it was done.

I normally appreciate advice and am always
happy enough when I am offered a free lesson
from people, but I knew his lessons were never
easily given. The intent of the evil task master
was to always shove it straight down my throat
repeatedly, all the while teaching me a lesson
instead of giving me one. The bigger his
audience, the more he enjoyed it.

He purposely stood close to me, waiting like
a ferocious predator stalking its timid prey,

perfectly timing the moment to strike with precision on my vulnerabilities and weaknesses. It was as if he prayed for me to fail or fall short, then erupted into glorious cheers when I did. I rarely disappointed him in his need to find fault and denigrate. It took me a while to realize I was his enemy. I needed to be knocked down at every available opportunity, or have my head used as a display trophy with each successive kill he made. I no longer saw us as being husband and wife. Instead, we became the hunter and the hunted.

While at the top of this ski run, after having endured another round of his precise instructions, I again wiped out on that berm which conquered more skiers than had conquered the challenge it presented. That was, of course, with him being the exception. And without fail, his moment of precision was immediate. The target was locked. The countdown on the timer had reached zero. Exterminate!

"GET UP AND GET GOING! YOU DIDN'T LISTEN TO A WORD I

At Least He Wasn't Hitting You...

*SAID, DID YOU? ONCE AGAIN,
YOU PURPOSELY DID THAT!
YOU'RE A TERRIBLE SKIER. YOU
CAN'T DO ANYTHING RIGHT!"*

There were people everywhere, watching and witnessing his unnecessary rage. Even now as I tell this story, my bones shudder and my skin crawls. It was blatant, public, verbal abuse. Again, nobody came to my rescue or dared to say something to him. Had camera phones been around at the time, I would have inadvertently become an overnight social media sensation - an object for people to cast judgement against, write comments about, dissect what they saw, call me a stupid cunt, or fire emojis of laughter, wow's, tears, or anger - whatever their choice might be. Anyone who is an abuser might even offer a thumbs-up symbol or feel I deserved what was being handed to my sorry, wretched ass. Perhaps they would even use a few choice words, most of which I had heard previously but never became numb to.

Every strike while the iron was hot burned into my blistered and raw flesh just as furiously as each successive time before. Since he'd scared everyone around us to the point they would be extremely foolish to voluntarily walk into his verbal shrapnel, they knew better and remained as bystanders since they too would have been lacerated in his primitive process to kill the prey standing before him. It was as if I was possessed and he needed to free me of the demons he thought had taken control of my soul. My exorcism was well underway.

I remember sitting in the snow that fateful day, wondering why my suicide solution hadn't worked. It would have been much better if my memory was nothing more than an epitaph on a lonely granite headstone, telling about the life of the deceased person below. Then again, I'm sure my husband would have wanted his words to make up the inscription instead of anything I desired.

> *"Can't Understand Normal Thinking! Herein lies a supposed "teacher". This bitch truly believed she was the perfect*

At Least He Wasn't Hitting You...

wife to me, the woman of her dreams. She turned out to be nothing but a useless fuck. She caused me tremendous grief. The stupid bitch wouldn't listen to anything I had to say. At Least I Wasn't Hitting Her... Rot In Purgatory, you fucking cunt!"

The craziest thing about the verbal abuse he directed towards me was if someone else had been making such degrading, grotesque and condescending statements toward me the way he did, he would have been incensed. His explosive anger would rival that of punishment beatings I'd learned about while watching Irish documentaries. If ever given the opportunity, he would relish in taking an individual down a dark alley, shooting them in each knee joint, separating their upper and lower legs, and laughing demonically as they crumble to the ground. But even if he were to become physically violent in such a way, it would not have been about punishment, it would have been about control, and rendering someone helpless to his demoralizing command.

On the other hand, not once did he string any kind of thought together about his horrendous abuse or the mouthfuls of shit his tongue shoveled in my direction. He would not tolerate it from anyone else, yet it was perfectly okay for him to be a raving, verbally-abusive, sociopathic lunatic who took pleasure in assaulting me day in and out. If he missed one day due to his work schedule, he sure as hell made up for it the next.

He was one sick, tormented bastard with countless internal demons. His anger decayed below the surface of his grey matter, becoming tremendously toxic and even more pungent since he added new ingredients of hatred into the already overflowing bucket of malice which consumed his thought processes. He could blow at any given moment. I was never able to keep my guard up high enough for it.

I could see, feel and sense when the perfect storm was coming. Even when I knew it was brewing and did my best to prepare, it was never enough. He was always stronger and more powerful than I could have ever imagined. His tongue cut me to shreds. The anger in his eyes burned holes in my soul. Laceration upon painful laceration inflicted upon my body with each verbal attack only festered as the wounds from the previous assault never healed. Perhaps it would have been better to be punched or kicked. At least hematomas eventually heal and broken bones mend. The verbal abuse served a completely different level of suffering. The scars from them affected every aspect of my sense of being, including my emotional, mental, physical, and spiritual.

Other times, he could turn on a dime. His rage and anger blindsided me as if someone had snuck up, knocked me down, and started unleashing thoughts as furious as punches. I would continually shake my head and wonder why he was doing this. Not only did the mutilation of my soul continue, the damage which had already been inflicted was beyond irreparable.

What I came to understand was NOTHING I tried to do was ever going to be good enough for him, no matter how hard I tried to be the best wife I could be, or to improve myself to prove to him the happiness he sought was with me. There was no way I would please him without an insult first being drilled into my skull.

I felt so incredibly helpless at his treatment of me. The wife he claimed to love. His partner in crime. The sparkle in his eye. A diamond in the rough. The twinkle in his star. No, I was none of those. I was a nobody. Not only was I nothing other than being a useless, worthless and unlovable cunt, I was *his* cunt. His to own. His to use. His to abuse. This is what I had become and distinguished myself as being. I was no longer a human being, or a woman.

He had cemented this thought into my mind, heart and soul. I stopped recognizing who I was and was completely disconnected and removed from the young lady I was brought up as. I was nothing more than his property to treat as he saw fit. I was his fucking pathetic, worthless little bitch which he could readily assault after every binge-drinking

At Least He Wasn't Hitting You...

session he engaged in. I was the recipient of his brutality whether we were behind closed doors or out in the open for all to hear and see. He pulled my puppet strings whenever and wherever he felt the need to make me dance for an audience.

The longer I stayed with him, the more clear it became, until one day I finally came to see that his perpetually malevolent face rarely smiled or softened its crimson tone. This was especially when I could not follow through on his strict lessons or instructions. The choice remained his.

I was nothing but a bucket overflowing with disposable sin. Not only did I marry, but I now belonged to an evil task master.

Chapter Twelve:
The Day the Music Died.

"You must find the place inside you where nothing is impossible."

- **Deepak Chopra**

When I was young, I took piano lessons for years. My mother was a fan of the clarinet so I ended up playing that as well. This was not by my own choice, but because she pushed me in this direction and was trying her best to refine me. Although I was drawn to percussion instruments, which of course included the drums, I took up the bass clarinet.

I had a working understanding of music, could both read and play it, but it wasn't my deal. I could do it but did not want to shine a spotlight on it. I was never interested in having my classmates or my teachers showcase this in music classes or on stage. I didn't like attention.

When I was in college, I briefly considered a minor degree in music. The only reason I did this is that deep down inside I knew I did not have the discipline to put the required hours in each day to further refine what I had already learned. My interests included participating in athletic activities such as track and field. I was a runner. I preferred to be outside in the sunshine, enjoying the fresh air while displaying my competitive streak rather than being locked up in a closet with a piano, prancing my fingers back and forth across the ivory keys. I remembered the freedom I felt when I ran, which was more pronounced than ever now. Where did that girl go, I wondered. The one who ran with wind in her hair, looking forward to the road ahead, to the future? The only running I wanted to do now was away from this loveless and abusive marriage.

During my marriage, we had a piano in the house. However, I was not allowed to play it while my husband was home. On one occasion, his mother became quite upset with him and asked why I was not allowed to play. He replied only that he didn't want to hear it and shut her down on the spot. That was the end of that conversation.

I now realize he was jealous. He hated that I actually did something better than him, which is why my piano playing set him off. If ever a weak spot of his became uncovered, he could not handle it or respect the talents of another. Yet he gave no mercy whatsoever when it came to him pointing out everyone else's flaws, including those who golfed or skied with him. He never wanted to be stood up or seen as being *less than* anyone else in any way.

At this stage, I was in my thirties and wanted to rekindle my abilities in music since I was no longer involved in athletic activities. When I was teaching, my students, along with some students from other grades at the school, had expressed interest in performing a Spring musical. I was asked to direct it. At first, the thought of this was extremely intimidating, but as we went along, it became an enjoyable and engaging experience. It helped me find strength and reminded me I had talents and abilities which weren't allowed to be expressed

At Least He Wasn't Hitting You...

in my home. It made me feel worthy. I was not just a teacher, but I was also not the dumb cunt I was led to believe I was through the never-ending pounding of verbal abuse from him. This reinforced a belief within me that I *could* make a difference in the lives of others.

My parents came to see the full production. They drove four hours across the state just to be in the audience. Of course, my husband was nowhere to be found. In retrospect, I am glad he was not there as I ended up receiving several accolades from community members who approached not only myself directly but also my parents to express their love and joy about what I had accomplished.

It was a surreal experience as I had gone from being a cunt a few days prior to directing my students through each of the musical numbers and having my picture in the newspaper. As we were in a good-sized city, the distribution of the community newspaper was large scale. I had not gone looking for attention, but it was lavished upon me nonetheless.

It was extremely strange for me to receive praise of any sort, especially at this stage of my life. I was so grateful and humbled, I thanked each person individually for taking the time to approach me.

Since this was happening, though, panic and fear began to rise in my mind because I knew the more accolades I received, the more I was going to be punished for it. My face was front and center for everyone to see. Although this was about me trying to find an outlet through music once again, as well as finding something fun to do in the community, it also meant I was not under the thumb of my husband. He was not behind the controls of this musical cockpit.

My husband became aware I was receiving widespread attention. Yet contrary to my previous experience with him, not once did he ask me how the production was coming along or acknowledge my face was in the paper along with several glowing reviews. He did not erupt into his usual tirade. Instead, he went silent. Not *one* word was muttered from the toxic

At Least He Wasn't Hitting You...

hole in his face, which was shocking to me to say the least. I expected otherwise. This was completely on the opposite end of the spectrum of his normal behavior.

As a result of his indifference, I stopped. Like a neglected child, I hoped he would suddenly notice me because I had done well. Instead, aware he couldn't convincingly argue against the rave reviews of dozens of strangers, for once, he strategically chose silence as a weapon, a weapon he knew would hurt me even more than words.

Except for doing a few small classroom activities with my students, I lost my passion to do anything musical thereafter. Looking back, I now know it was more than just lack of approval from him that made me quit, it was the complete absence of frivolity and joy in my soul. And for me, those had always been the two ingredients from which music emanates. My piano became a piece of furniture, serving absolyno purpose other than to collect dust.

Along with another piece of my heart, that was the day the music died.

Chapter Thirteen:

Raging.

"The loudest one in the room is the weakest one in the room."

- **Frank Lucas**

My husband's rage was pervasive in all aspects of our married life. He certainly refined this method over a period of many years, long before he met me. As I look back at our marriage and at him, I see a man who was consumed by demons. I don't think even he knew about the demons that were in his mind, nor could he acknowledge or explain them.

I know he drank to escape from them, but because he never could, the ultimate outcome was swinging his machete-like rage at everyone and everything, especially me since I was convenient, available, and didn't fight back for the most part against the verbal assaults unleashed upon me by him. It was not my style

At Least He Wasn't Hitting You...

to name-call and fly into rages. It was not my style to pick a fight. By nature, I am not a fighter but a lover.

A friend of his came in from out of town once to play in a golf tournament with him. The fellow was nice enough, so there was no problem in having him stay at our residence.

I had been working all day and arrived home shortly after my shift ended. He and his friend arrived two hours later. They were extremely intoxicated as there was no limit to how much they should have drank regardless of who was driving them home. And as usual, anything I said or did, or something I didn't say or do, put my husband into an explosive rage. This quickly escalated into a full verbal assault. However, this was an extremely rare occasion because he rarely ever took his rage to this level when someone was in our home.

But also extremely rare was my reaction. In the middle of this fresh tirade, something within me snapped again. Like the dinner party years before, the only other time I had ever stood up to him in front of others, I decided it was again time to take a stand and rush headlong into the battle in a way he would understand. I started yelling at HIM, telling him EXACTLY what I thought. I didn't hold back the long-suppressed tidal wave of words!

The look on his friend's face was one of unadulterated shock. I felt bad that he had to hear and witness any part of it even though every other time I was the only audience member and recipient. Even in full drunken stupor, it was quite evident his friend felt pure shame for helping establish this moment. Perhaps it was shame for helping my husband become so extraordinarily intoxicated.

Unfortunately, none of my pent-up frustrations fazed my husband in the slightest. He continued with his ranting rage so much I finally had had enough. I made my move and was getting ready to leave when he grabbed all of the cars keys from the counter and said I wasn't going anywhere because I did not own either car.

His blatant attempt to block me didn't deter me. I'd had enough. I exited out the side door and began walking down the street, trying my damn best to formulate a plan. It was certainly not my intention to have the fight of the century that evening. It was not my intention to embarrass the guest in our home. Nor was it ever my intention to upset both of our dogs and leave them as frightened and bewildered as our house guest was. But I had to do something. It was dark and late. I had nowhere to go and no money on me. Jumbled thoughts tumbled around in my tormented mind.

I considered going to a neighbor's house, but we hadn't been living in Texas very long at this point so I wasn't close to any of them, at least not close enough to let them in on our dysfunctional world.

I ended up at a nearby elementary school, sitting in an outside stairwell at the back of the building. At the time, it was the best I could do. I sat in the dark except for the faint, depressing glow of an exterior security light.

Not only was I by myself in the dark, I felt completely alone in this world. Anguished, betrayed, deceived, abandoned, defeated, abused. Every gut-wrenching feeling of pure despair and desperation I experienced in my marriage boiled and spilled over the surface that night.

I sat and cried my eyes out like I had never cried before. I was finally a broken woman, one without hope or direction as to where my life was heading.

As I sat on those steps, I thought of the word marriage and what it was supposed to mean. There was absolutely nothing about this marriage that came anywhere close to resembling the connection between a wife and her husband. Partners. Lovers. Soulmates. Regardless of whatever socially-constructed terminology is used to describe the bonded yet 'holy' union of matrimony between woman and man, our marriage meant nothing to me at this point. What it was can be truly described as a symphony of human destruction. Every fiber within my very being had been shredded to pieces.

Before I took my partner's hand to become as one, I only had my parents' marriage to look

At Least He Wasn't Hitting You...

upon as a beautiful example. I'd never been down a path of wedded bliss before. One thing for certain is there was nothing blissful about it. Nor was it up for any sort of measurement or award for the perfect couple of the year. There is no other way to describe this other than to say I knew my situation was way, WAY beyond comprehension!

Recalling this story twenty years later, I still cry when I think of the fear and gamut of emotions I felt that dreadful night. The scarring remains but this story must and will be told.

After crying and falling asleep for a short time, I woke up and had a frightening feeling I needed to get the hell out of there.

As I sat alone in that dark and secluded stairwell, I felt very vulnerable to anyone who might come along and use this same spot as a place to shoot toxins into their veins or try and take advantage of me. As I had already endured an indescribable evening of verbal abuse, I did not want to make the situation worse by being exposed to physical or sexual assault. My mind was racing. I had to get out of there.

It was beyond any measurement of sadness and so incredibly defeating for me to finally realize that, though I was avoiding my home and husband, ending up on the streets was the safest, healthiest, and best alternative! A home is supposed to be a place of comfort, a refuge from the cruel world, but mine had become the cruelest place in the world.

I deserted my husband that night. The same man who stood under the watchful eyes of God, in front of many witnesses, who had gathered to hear him promise to love, honor, cherish and protect me. Not once did this happen in our ten years of marriage.

I reminded myself of that as the night air grew colder, and as I watched soft, warm, welcoming, yellow light and laughter emanating from houses across the street from the school – happy homes filled with people who cared about each other; homes that friends could come to and feel comfortable and

At Least He Wasn't Hitting You...

safe; homes where couples said I love you to each other every day, and meant it.

As I sat on the cold steps, the darkness of night mirroring the growing darkness within me, I wondered when I might wake up only to find myself in a cold sweat, realizing it was all a horrible dream. Here I was on the street, running away from my home, my place of sanctity, to escape the recurring nightmare which had become my reality.

I had no idea what time it was, but I snuck back over to my house only to discover that most of the lights had been turned off. There was no signs of anyone being up or about. Perhaps this was the chance I had been waiting for. Maybe the drunk bastard and his companion had kept on drinking and were now passed out from their intoxication. All I knew was I was not going to go back inside of my house. I couldn't sneak past my dogs without them barking and possibly waking my husband. Besides, he had already locked me out!

What I do know, however, is that I didn't have it in me to engage in another drunken argument with him. I now know the feeling people get when they are on the verge of snapping. If he would have started in on me again, there's no telling what I would have done. As much as I may have wanted to, there was no way I could take a chance or allow myself to go into a state of blind rage.

I went into the backyard of our home and slept on a lawn chair by the pool. It was fenced and private so I felt as safe as I was ever going to feel that night. The emotional upheaval always exhausted me, but this particular night's was multiplied to the power of exponential levels. It was beyond measurement. My last thought as I drifted off to sleep was about how angry my parents and family, especially my brothers, would be at how viciously my husband was treating me. They never knew what I was going through or when I was going through it. I felt so ashamed about all of it. It was as if *I* was the perpetrator of all the abuse. I am sure one of my brothers would have come to my rescue, if only I had reached out to him.

The following morning, while in a state of complete exhaustion, I finally decided to make my way back into our house. I expected the worse, but not a single word was mentioned about the violent rage which had occurred the previous evening.

Nothing.

Chapter Fourteen:
Painted into a Corner.

"Whenever you feel unloved, unimportant or insecure, remember to whom you belong."

- **Ephesians 2: 19-22**

Even after that horrendous night, I didn't leave. Hope really does spring eternal. Like every other abused woman in the world who doesn't walk out, choosing the freedom of homelessness over hell, I kept thinking, hoping and praying that somehow, some way, he would change. I see very clearly now how foolish I was, but only because of the clarity of hindsight. In real time, people get stuck. I mean flat tires with weeds grown up around them stuck. I mean opening the rusty hood and seeing that the entire engine is missing stuck.

It didn't need to be an explosive event for my husband to try to shun me at every

At Least He Wasn't Hitting You...

opportunity or control my every move. At home, he had zero impulse control. In fact, I often wondered how he could be such a raving lunatic at home and a cool professional at work – how he could get behind the cockpit of an airplane and not go postal. Lord knows everything I did was met with massive headaches and challenges no matter how large or little the task was.

Even though I slept by our swimming pool the night before, he decided he wanted it pulled up out of the ground and turned in a different direction. I figured it was his intention to disrupt my only refuge since the backyard would be in construction chaos, preventing me from being able to sleep out there on the nights when fights like this occurred. I saw it as a waste of money but he was so annoyed that I slept by the pool and out of his circle of control, he was determined to cut that option off for me forevermore.

Having the pool cleaned became *my* responsibility, which wasn't much of a change because he never did much to look after it himself before. On top of that, I could not do laundry to *his* standards, nor could I keep the house clean enough. I was working just as much as he was, perhaps more since he had to have down time as a pilot. Yet he could set the autopilot to fly the plane for him. He was there simply to do what he did best: watch and make sure the controls followed his command. The house wasn't much different.

Trying to get a compliment out of him was like Bob Cratchit asking for another shilling from Ebenezer Scrooge. He hated being home yet he both demanded me to do all the housework and wait on him hand and foot for his every need. It was a constant mind game trying to figure out what he wanted or needed.

He never made dinner for me on the days when he was home and I was out at work. I did not dare to make this a gripe with him as it would have been another fight. However, I prepared him supper one night and after he was done, since he had said nothing to me about the meal he had happily consumed, I

At Least He Wasn't Hitting You...

asked for his thoughts. I should have known better.

"It's okay. Mine's better."

So much for me trying to make his life easier. I was never going to get anywhere with him no matter how hard I tried.

One time I came home from work and opened the garage door to find the kitchen sink sitting in the middle of the floor. My husband had taken it upon himself to paint the kitchen and failed to ask me what my thoughts were on this. There was no discussion. It was *his* kitchen though he rarely cooked in it. It was *his* sink though he refused to wash any dishes. And it was *his* paint to do with as he pleased. I knew better to not ask and just get out of his way.

While we were living in the Midwest, he suddenly decided we were moving to Guam. Since it was in the middle of the Pacific Ocean, he felt he could make all sorts of money flying between different islands. He also decided I was going to teach at the local naval and Air

Force base. After that plan died, he decided we were going to move to Saudi Arabia where he would not have to pay taxes on his earnings. He seemed to relish the fact that women had no rights in that country. Especially me.

His manic and depressive states would swing violently from one end of the spectrum to the other. When he was in this mode, he refused to shower and would wear the same clothes for days at a time. At one point, he refused to even get off the couch. He would sit watching TV shows, especially world news, which would make him stew at the events going on around the world, the ashtray overflowing all the while.

He became angry at me when I got the vacuum cleaner out because he couldn't hear the TV. He rarely vacuumed but would ask me when I last changed the vacuum bag. Every single time. When he did use it, he would leave it out for me to put away and would complain if I didn't. Anything he could think of to start a fight.

He wanted to open a bagel store when we lived in the Midwest. He was doing all the planning for it as if it would ever really happen. The biggest decision he made, however, without any consultation from me, was that he was going to quit being a pilot and attend medical school. Usually, it's better to have an in-depth conversation with one's spouse before making life-changing decisions like this, but he did not seem to see it this way.

He never took into consideration what money was required to purchase items. There was zero engagement with him. It was his money. For instance, he once purchased a large-screen projection TV. Of course, it was one of his deals - when I came home, there it was waiting for me to see. He often bought expensive items whether I wanted him to or not. I learned to not voice my displeasure about him doing things such as this because when I did, his standard response was, *"I can afford it."*

That was his justification for buying everything impulsively. A well thought out purchase was rare. Yet if I were to bring home a shirt or a pair of shoes, I would be interrogated as if I had entered the codes for nuclear war without prior consultation.

What was most interesting is he never called me any brutal, derogatory names when he was manic. There was rarely any middle ground.

However, on one occasion, and I do mean "one" occasion, he was an absolutely delightful person. Unfortunately, this only occurred because he had an accident and was pumped full of morphine, which allowed him to let his guard down and stop being so sadistic. It was the only time I ever got any reprieve and respite from his mouth. Sadly, those were some of the best days we ever had together. The morphine made him a charming person. He was tolerant, sweet, funny, polite and I found I could live with him without having my throat cut by his words. We watched television together and he laughed heartily, something

At Least He Wasn't Hitting You...

else that had always been lacking in his personality.

Then came the end of the drugs. It was painfully obvious to the medical community he was a chronic alcoholic due to the levels of morphine they had to administer to him to help manage the pain from his accident. This sent him into aggressive sweats from the withdrawal and made him worse and more impulsive than ever before.

I found it more pleasant to go to work than to be around him while he was detoxing. It was only then that I realized I'd been painted into a corner.

Chapter Fifteen:
One Final Straw.

"I set myself free from the past and I forgive everyone who participated in it."

- **Iyanla**

Just before I finally left my husband and moved into my own apartment, I was still living with him at our house. One lazy Sunday afternoon, he was watching golf or some other sporting event on TV. I was getting ready to go grocery shopping and had written out a list of items.

I asked him three times if there was anything he needed. I didn't dare ask if he wanted to go with me as he was so engrossed in the program. This was his routine and nothing new to me. My gut told me no matter what I decided to buy for him, it was going to be wrong and he would want something different after I got home.

At Least He Wasn't Hitting You...

He finally responded and said he couldn't think of anything. Truth be told, he didn't care because it would have taken him away from his program. His response was mechanical and without thought.

I went ahead and did the shopping. After arriving home, I started to unpack the bags only to be suddenly met in the kitchen by him. I knew he was about to launch into one of his devastating personal attacks on me but was trying to use stealthy tactics to surprise me. He asked me in an all-knowing tone, licking his chops and preparing for the first strike.

"Did you get any coke?"

I immediately said I did not. I told him I had asked if he wanted or needed something and each time he told me he couldn't think of anything. Hearing this only threw him into a greater rage.

"I TOLD you I wanted COKE!"

The three times I asked him, the only word he said to me was no. It wasn't yes. Nor was there a maybe or perhaps. There was no request for him to take a second or two to think about it or to wait for the play to end before offering up his thoughts. Yet I knew he was going to lay into me as if he was a UFC fighter coming in for the knockout punch.

Sure enough, he landed the first blow, but this was just the start. A tirade of words immediately followed in straight succession. Strike after jaw-breaking strike.

"You bitch. You fucking bitch. All you think about is yourself. Do you know what you are? You are one lazy, selfish, fucking cunt!"

The words continued lashing down upon me like a torrential rainstorm. Once again, I would be cut to shreds by his razor-sharp tongue. The problem was that I had not read his mind about what he wanted. It was not about him telling me he wanted coke. I should have known by his "do not disturb" body language before leaving for the store that what he really wanted was to attack me for something, anything.

He started by endlessly repeating I only thought of myself. It was as if I had been hit across the head yet again. Even though I tried to prepare myself in advance on the way home from the store, knowing full-well this was likely going to happen, I could not have prepared enough.

That afternoon and evening, he asked me out to dinner. There was no apology first because, in his mind, he had done nothing wrong. I was the one who was at fault.

We went to a 1950's style diner where we could order food while remaining in the vehicle. Although we did not have a convertible at this time, it seemed he wanted to make it up to me for his latest verbal assault by giving me this unique dining experience. However, it quickly became clear that he was more interested in showing everyone in the car park around us that he was taking his sweetheart out for dinner, being a perfect gentleman, showing everyone else how it was done. If only they knew the truth.

I wonder what I looked like that night. I'm sure my face looked as if I had just emerged from a foxhole, a beleaguered soldier fighting a bloody yet senseless war. There was no apology from him. Surrounded by happy energy and 50's music, I should have been happy, but I was completely lost. As I stared into space and tried to clear the fog, this thought came to my mind, clearer than ever.

> *"I am fucking done with this. Once and for all. It is time for me to stop dreaming and fantasizing he'll leave me alone or, better yet, die!"*

This feeling was even stronger than the night in the dark stairwell. Maybe because we were somewhere happy and alive, with couples around us who truly enjoyed each other. The contrast between this place and my actual world did more to make me aware of how far I had fallen than the dark stairwell ever could – because there was actually very little difference - my life felt like a dark stairwell all the time.

I was angry at myself for falling into my comfort zone again. The thing about comfort

At Least He Wasn't Hitting You...

zones most people don't realize is they don't need to be comfortable. "Comfortable" is whatever one has gotten used to. That's why abuse can be passed down through generations. Human beings are very adaptive, so much so that they can sometimes adapt to a life that's extremely unhealthy.

The push was finally on to save enough money to become financial independent and break free from this evil bastard once and for all. There was no turning back this time. I knew I wouldn't be able to walk into our home one day and say I was leaving, pack my bags, and move out. It would take some careful planning on my behalf to get out of there, and I needed to do it under a veil of total secrecy. Otherwise, one of two things would happen - either he would be completely charming to me while telling me everything was going to be fine and that he realized his mistakes, or he would erupt from the depths of hell and condemn me for all damnation, most likely the latter. The devil likes his servants to be obedient. There was no training required since I had already been molded by him. As much as it hurt, I eventually became callused to him calling me a fucking cunt.

I had anticipated this day. I did not know when or how it might come, but it had. I just knew within my heart, with every single beat, every step I took, and every breath I drew, I was closer to the end of his desecration of me.

Then the final straw I had been waiting for made its debut appearance.

As Greg will tell you from his time in the Faculty of Human Ecology prior to entering Social Work, leading researchers working in the field of domestic and family violence have published reports which state abused women will say they are going to leave their relationship and tormentor an average of thirty-six times before they finally find enough strength and courage to make their move.

Looking back, I realize I was likely among the countless numbers of abused and battered women who were not counted within the data captured by those statistics.

Remember I said abuse can be both visible and invisible? The abuse and violence which occurs behind closed doors often goes unreported. Therefore, unfortunately, it is quite likely the actual number of abused persons is much larger than has been reported. I am not alone. Neither are you.

Chapter Sixteen:

A Great Escape.

"Everything you want is on the other side of fear."

- **Jack Canfield**

After the final straw, I knew I had to get out once and for all. As much as I was afraid to go backward, the thought of moving forward also terrified me. Anxiety filled my body from head to toe. I was extremely intimated by the thought of getting out, but my heart and soul told me I wasn't going to be able to last much longer. It was do or die. Although I had tried to take my own life, I was not about to let *him* take it for me. I decided he was not going to control my exit from this earth. There was no other alternative.

To summon the strength to do this felt impossible yet it had to be done. I was determined to be proactive about this but had

At Least He Wasn't Hitting You...

to be stealthy to avoid tipping him off. My research was done secretly. If he found out about it, he would've gone into an uncontrollable rage to get me back under his thumb again.

Financially, it was easy for me to pull it all together because I kept a separate bank account from him. He never knew how much money I had in my account just as much as I was unaware of what he had in his.

While he was out on one of his trips, I searched for and secured an apartment for myself. It was in the same neighborhood but far enough from him that he wouldn't know where I was. The place was brand new and gated. The landlord offered free rent for the first and last month, with no damage deposit. We were a perfect match. They were eager to bring tenants in and I was eager to be free of my husband. This felt like a financial godsend because it allowed me to stretch my savings much further.

I made the arrangements and was ready to go when he came home from a trip. He immediately wanted to go look at a motor home which cost well over a quarter million dollars. He explained his reasoning behind this:

"I have flown all over the country, but in my retirement years I want to actually see what this place looks like."

The thought of this was nauseating because I was trying to get away from this man and he was planning for a future with him. My response was articulate but blunt.

"I don't want to go and look at those. I don't see my future being with you."

There are times in life when you wish you had a camera handy. If I had a photo of his face at that moment, I would enlarge it, frame it and hang it on the wall. The smug bastard actually thought I would be excited about many more decades of his abuse, or perhaps the novelty of being yelled at in a rolling home instead of a stationary one for a change. Maybe he thought the pretty scenery would make constantly devastating my soul more palatable.

At Least He Wasn't Hitting You...

Suffice to say he looked like I had just smacked him across the face with a dead fish.

In my mind, it was insane to buy a motor home. But again, this was *his* dream and decision. I was not consulted on this purchase and did not want to be party to it. It was tough enough living in a house with him, even with him gone for long periods at a time, but moving into a motor home meant I would find myself living in an even smaller goldfish bowl with the piranha.

Again, he was being impulsive because he took a shine to some new toy he wanted. His manic-depressive mood swings were probably to blame. He would spend money to make himself happy one day then become depressed and drink himself into oblivion again the next. If he had not brought up the camper, I could have slipped away as I had planned. Now I had to explain myself.

> *"This should come as no surprise to you. I am unhappy. I have not been happy for years because of how you have treated me, spoken to me, and*

cut me to the bone with the names you call me. My heart is not in this marriage anymore. As far as I'm concerned, it's over."

His response was a shock to me as I was expecting a full-on verbal assault. All he said was:

"Please don't leave while I'm away on a trip."

In my mind, this was a kind of "checkmate" move on his part, as if we were playing a real-life game of chess. I knew what I was going to say but foolish words formed in my brain and came out before I could stop them.

"I promise you I will not leave you while you are on a trip."

Once again, a scene unfolded in my mind, but it was different this time because we were having an adult conversation for the first time in years. It's a good thing my heart was in a better state of being than my mind was. But even as I made that promise, I knew I would have to break it and leave him when he was

At Least He Wasn't Hitting You...

gone because there was no way he would let me out the front door alive.

Within the next week or two, my husband once again departed for the friendly skies. I checked to see what his flight schedule was. This way, I knew he would be far away when I put my plan into action.

I contacted a friend and asked him to help me move. He came by a few hours later with three friends. I didn't leave the house until the day I knew he was coming home so the dogs wouldn't be left for alone for too long.

I wrote a note which simply said this:

"I have moved out. I am gone."

There was nothing else to say. There was no point in going into detail as I knew I'd receive a phone call as soon as he read the seven words I wrote on that piece of paper. Immediately thereafter, I went to my apartment and sat alone. He did not have a forwarding address for me, nor did I let him know where I was going to be, so a face-to-face confrontation was not going to occur. The dread of staring at my cell phone, anticipating that call, was beyond nerve-racking.

Eventually, he called. The first words out of his mouth were:

"YOU promised you were not going to leave while I was away. YOU broke your promise! What do YOU have to say for YOURSELF?"

Once again, his tones were menacing, only this time I did not feel the need to carefully calculate my response. I had a lot to say but didn't need much to get my viewpoint across to him. There was no point in rehashing everything that had gone on for years. I instead tried to be respectful yet let him know that *I* was now in control. Finally, the tables had turned.

"I can't take it anymore. I can't take any of this. The marriage. The abuse. The spiteful name-calling. Constantly walking on eggshells

At Least He Wasn't Hitting You...

and not being good enough. I'm done with it. I am done with you!

I begged you for years to get help. I asked you to please stop what you were doing. You refused to listen. I tried telling you how I felt. When you treat your spouse this way, this happens. This is not my fault this time. You are to blame."

At that point, since I had spelled everything out for him, he said he wanted to give *me* space so *I* could cool off, think everything through properly with a clear mind, and reconsider the decision *I* made. He tried to turn the tables back in his favor by saying *I* was the one who needed time to realize the mistake *I* was making in leaving *him*. However, to my surprise, he respected my decision. His suggestion that I "think it over" made it obvious to me his head was in the clouds.

After concluding our discussion, he ended the call and left me alone. Three months passed. Three months that were sometimes scary and lonely but wonderfully, beautifully free of abuse. The rebuilding of myself had begun, which included excavation of who I was before I met him.

The night I left him, he went away a wounded man. For the first time in his life, he finally felt what it was like to have pain shoved down his throat, a knife stuck into his heart, a slap across his face, and what it felt like to be human and experience real emotions. Yet all of them paled in comparison to the damages I had suffered for years at his bastard hands.

I had finally made my great escape.

Chapter Seventeen:
The Separation.

"The hardest battle you are ever going to have to fight is that battle to be just you."

- **Leo Buscaglia**

At thirty-six years of age, I had moved into my first apartment as an adult. Other than those I lived in as a student while going to college, I was now twice the age I was when I got my first apartment. It left me with an eerily familiar feeling of helplessness as this was exactly how I felt when I left my parents' house for the first time. It was as if I had returned from the frontline battle trenches, fighting in a war zone and trying to decompress, deprogram myself, and shake off the dust from what I had just emerged.

The feeling of being free for the first time in years did not come easy. It took some time for me to acclimate to my new surroundings without worrying about preparing myself for another rage blindside. A loop tape kept playing in my head telling me I was a cunt and did not deserve to be out here on my own. I kept pondering if I was prepared, capable, or deserving of this. I had become my own worst enemy. It was an agonizing struggle trying to separate my current sense of reality from the effects of the abuse.

I was working, trucking along and staying busy. My friends and family knew I was separated but not once did they dare ask me what happened since they knew about him and his behavior. During this time, I had a health scare, which was quite frightening since I was alone and had no one there to help me.

Not only had I been alone in my marriage, but felt I was all alone in the world since I had no one. It was not as if I would have had any help from my husband since he had abandoned me when I went under the knife for a D&C and left me on the floor to die when I tried to commit suicide. I should have been used to being alone.

It was December of 1999. I had remained mostly alone for those first three months. Maybe it was a period of mourning of everything that might have been. But it was also a rebirth of what could be.

I began making plans to live life again and started calling friends to ask them to go out and have some fun. I had confined myself to my apartment. The outside world was my enemy. I even worried that he had perhaps hired a private plane to fly around our area to see if he could spot my car or me. It was not an outlandish idea. I mean, he had considered moving an entire swimming pool so I would have no place on the property to sleep after a fight. There was nothing he wouldn't do to keep me under his control.

Although I was free from his clutches, I was still afraid of being grabbed, stuffed into the trunk of his car, and taken hostage within our home. What was not evident to me was that his programming was so deep and engrained, I couldn't even trust my own mind anymore. I was torn between the new life I was now living and the vows I had exchanged with my husband under the watchful eyes of God.

Just as things were getting comfortable for me living as a single woman, my husband called again. He had somehow convinced himself that he'd had an epiphany and was ready to rekindle our relationship. Simply put, he wanted back in. I wasn't ready to re-engage with him. I didn't even want to hear his voice. I told him I wasn't interested but he kept calling. Although he did not come out and say it directly, I knew he wanted to take control of the reins again, and me.

If he would have told me that he had seen a psychologist, it would have meant he spent money for someone to get through to him he required serious help. This would entail several (thousand) therapy sessions. I knew this was never going to be the case. Had I of said this to him, it would have put him over the edge.

Although I was struggling with my decision to leave and was still angry with him, I thought that perhaps therapy was not a bad thing for him because he would learn how his explosive

At Least He Wasn't Hitting You...

behavior triggered so easily. I hoped therapy would help him take a solid look at how he engaged with the people in his life and understand why I decided to walk out. My hope for his recovery and growth surprised and disturbed me. After all, I had every right to hate him and wish he was dead. My mind was more tormented than I first realized.

But instead of seeking honest analysis, which would have made him feel too vulnerable, he sought ways which were more in tune with his belief that he could fix anything, including himself and me. This did not include individual or couple therapy. No, he merely read a book and proclaimed his eyes were fully opened and that he saw things in a different light. He clung to the thought that the advice of some stranger was going to cure everything, get us back together, and resolve nine years of abuse as if it were a magical pill.

Open up and say ahh. Wonderful.

What he failed to realize is I was more than well-aware of his game and wasn't falling into that trap ever again. At his request, we met at a bar to speak about what he had learned. I saw through everything he presented and was not ready or willing to return to any of it. Had I done so and followed his direction, I would have been better off slitting my own throat.

Separation was now the name of my game.

Chapter Eighteen:
Cold Hard Steel.

"Dearly beloved, we are all gathered here today to get through this thing called life."

- **Prince**

During our meeting at the bar, my husband asked me to give up my apartment and move back in with him. He suggested that my living standard must be drastically worse and tried to use the comfort of our home as a lure. He even tried to convince me of how lonely I must be without him. I told him I enjoyed the solitude after so many horrible years and that life in my one-bedroom apartment was peaceful and more than adequate to meet my needs. Having a fancy home was not all it was cracked up to be, especially because there was nowhere to hide from his taunts and verbal assaults. For the first time in almost ten years, I could come home to predictability, one without torture or surprise.

I told him I wasn't interested in his suggested arrangement. He countered this by saying he needed someone he trusted to look after our dogs while he was away on long trips.

Why he wanted me back was beyond me since he showed nothing but loathing and distrust of me when I was living with him. But my love for our dogs pulled on my heartstrings. I knew they were not the ones to cause me undue grief when I arrived home each day from work. They were there to welcome me, tails wagging, panting heavily while showing looks of excitement and jumping up to hug me.

I finally relented. When he was gone on his trips, I went to our house and took care of the dogs. After work, I headed back to ensure they had not made a mess. When my husband was due to come back from each trip, I would leave early and seek sanctuary in my own apartment to avoid unnecessary contact.

Each week, I would move into our house for two or three days. The dogs were confused but happy I was there to take care of them. Since I let my husband back into my life on a limited basis, this went on for a period of five months. Just as had occurred after casting my ballot in the gubernatorial election, I finally relented to his persistent questioning. The one difference being and although I knew it wasn't in my best interests, I told him where I was residing.

So long as he did not expect me to live with him on a full-time basis, I was okay with this arrangement. He could no longer abuse me, dictate to me the direction my life was to take, or assault me with his sadistic choice of words. What was most surprising was we got along during this time. It was as if we were dating once again, with him acting like a nice, proper, young man making a wonderful impression.

His charade did not last long. A few weeks after the turn of the millennium, I learned my father had been diagnosed with a tumor on his pituitary gland. He had passed out at home. He was brought to the emergency room and assessed. Although I was informed these are rarely cancerous, he needed to undergo surgery immediately.

I recall leaving my job in Texas for a few days to go be at my father's side. I did not want my husband there because my family knew we were apart, but he insisted on going with me to see my family, and tried to present himself as a nice, supportive and pleasant fellow, though my family knew how he really was. Since he wouldn't stop badgering me and refused to take no for an answer, I relented. I wish I hadn't.

It was as if he couldn't bear the strain of being nice, even if he was just pretending, because he "reverted back to form" shortly after arriving, going back to his usual antics and ignorant displays. This included chain smoking and bragging to my brother about his Corvette. But I was too worried about my father to care about my husband's head games. The surgeons had gone through the roof of my father's mouth and into his skull. The gravity

At Least He Wasn't Hitting You...

of that situation dwarfed my husband's tired nonsense.

When I thought I had seen it all, he went so low as to use my father's operation as a way to get back into my world and pretend to be a supportive husband. But I was not bending to his will or playing his game. It did not work. We returned to Texas and went our separate ways with the same arrangement as before.

In March of 2000, I entered the back door only to be met with a surprise sitting on the dryer - a loaded .357 Magnum on full display. There was no other reason for it being there other than to send me the message if I ever tried to mess with him, the first bullet in the chamber would end up squarely between my eyes. No questions asked. Guilty until proven innocent.

Knowing his explosive nature, I'm certain he would have reloaded a few times and shot several more rounds into me to make sure I was dead before delivering his usual tirade of names into my face, screaming to know why I forced his hand and made him kill me.

As if a foreboding premonition, the scene played out in my head of what was coming:

"Look at what you made me do! You pathetic, motherfucking, dumbass, liberal-loving, stupid cunt! Had you listened to me in the first place, I wouldn't have shot you! Such a despicable bitch. Here, have another one. **BANG!**

Jesus fucking Christ! What the fuck. Look at the mess of your face, cunt. Did you forget our wedding vows? All you needed to do was listen! Fucking obey and serve me! That's all you had to do. OBEY ME! Until death do we part! **BANG!**

Why the fuck would you push me this far and force me to kill you? Such a stupid motherfucker you are! Why the fuck should I have to spend MY hard-earned money on YOUR pathetic funeral? You want to know what I think of that? **BANG! BANG!**

At Least He Wasn't Hitting You...

Who the fuck am I kidding? No one cares about you! I'll watch you burn in the crematorium. You'll continue to BURN IN HELL, you thoughtless, liberal-loving, fucking cunt! BANG!"

The message was plain and simple. He had a gun and was not afraid to use it. Even if it was purchased for self-defense, the dealer would have informed him to keep it in a safe area of the home, such as the bedroom, not on a dryer or in a place where it could be used *against* him if an intruder were to break in. Unless the gun was purchased solely for me. He never once hit me, but I could not rule out the possibility that he could unload a chamber of full metal jackets into my body.

Can anyone ever really know what another person is capable of, especially when that person has lost his most prized possession? Not me. Control. Control was everything to him. Power. Domination. He had lost them all. What might he do to get them back?

It was quite possible he sought out firing ranges while in other towns and cities to hone his skills. He never shared with me what he did during his downtime. Since he bragged about everything else, he likely also considered himself to be an expert marksman who could shoot any target from miles away while blindfolded.

Not once during our marriage did he ever have a gun on display. To my knowledge, he never had one in the house, nor did he have a license to carry or own one. Yet this was on the dryer, in plain sight, five feet from the back door. He probably thought he was sending a very clear message to me that he was still in control and had the upper hand. He probably thought he was re-establishing his authority. But all I saw was pathetic weakness, and all I felt was justification for leaving him.

I looked at it as his way of taking his game to the next level. I had broken away from him and established a sense of independence while trying to rebuild my life but he wanted me back in the house, not because he was lonely or needed someone to look after the dogs but because he wanted someone to control. I was

At Least He Wasn't Hitting You...

the most vulnerable target he had influence over.

He used the gun as an extension of *his* authority. I was *his* property. *His* to control. *His* to own. And even though I was living elsewhere, I was *still* bound by the strings he had tied me up with the day I took his hand in holy matrimony.

He was hoping the sight of his gun would make me shiver with fear that any challenge to his authority would end up with him sticking the cold, hard, steel barrel of his .357 Magnum into my mouth, cocking it, pulling the trigger and spreading my brains all over the walls of our house.

It was obviously a calculated plan on his part to make sure I saw the gun that day. If I was not going to be *his* bitch and fucking cunt, no one else was going to have me, either. After all, I was his property. He couldn't have some other man treating me right and trying to convince me that I was none of those horrible names he called me. That would undo all of his hard work.

Chapter Nineteen:

Exodus

"Do what you feel in your heart to be right – for you'll be criticized anyway."

- **Eleanor Roosevelt**

Studies have shown that individuals who experience several years of conditioning depart from all sense of logical thinking. Each year, millions of Americans are trapped in emotionally abusive relationships. I was one such case.

I had heard of Stockholm Syndrome before, in which an emotional relationship develops between an abused person and their captor. I never thought I would fall into that category. Yet the voices in my head continued telling me I was nothing without my husband. He was successful in his grooming of me. As was said in our wedding vows, until death do us part. He was determined to see this through even if it meant he was the cause of my death due to his reckless behavior.

A prime example of this is that after the gun incident, we ended up together at his house. Even after all he had done to destroy me, I still felt very sympathetic towards him and wanted to give him another chance to make his many wrongs right. But it was not on me to do this for him. I even thought that perhaps the book he had read on how to fix himself had indeed worked.

He made dinner for me, and although I chose to not drink anything alcoholic so that I could keep my wits about me, he was having a few drinks, as usual.

Everything was going well until I said something he didn't agree with. I knew what was coming. He snapped.

"You aren't even trying. If you aren't going to try and make this work, what the fuck are you even doing here?"

It was obvious that his sole intention was to get me back into his house, into bed, and under his control again and all this small talk was just an annoyance to him. All the making nice was surely a terrible strain. He was being nice to me, but when I realized his natural inclination was to lash out and go back to his old ways without actually wanting to make the changes he promised he would make based upon the book he had read, I realized the alleged life-changing book had either never been read or changed nothing.

"You're right, I don't need to be here."

I put down my cutlery, packed up, and walked out.

After that night, it was not just a separation, it was on to divorce court. I was determined to be free of the hell in which I had spent the last nine years of my life.

When I arrived back to my apartment that night, I settled in to a bath to try and wash away his latest verbal attack.

In May of 2000, at the end of the school year, I received word that my father needed another surgery. My ex-husband was out of my life at that point, in the background, Thankfully, he did not insist on coming with me this time. Since he told me to "get the fuck out" of his life and stop wasting his time, I no longer served any purpose to him. In fact, we stopped speaking entirely.

I decided to return to my childhood home to help my father and try to get him out of the hospital and back in his own home, but the surgeons told me cranial surgery required more recuperation time. My father wanted to go home and mow the lawn along with his usual chores but there was no way I was going to allow that to happen.

While staying with my parents, it dawned on me that I needed to get the hell out of Texas once and for all. When I did leave for the final time, there simply would be no turning back since there was nothing for me to return to. I had to get completely away from him, and only great distance could accomplish that.

After coming back to my family, I found a teaching job. I remained there feeling my life had returned to normal – the good, healthy normal I knew before meeting him - and the horrors were behind me once and for all. I was with my family, my real family, back where it all began, feeling like I had finally broken away and rediscovered life. My exodus from my tormentor, my demon, and my crucifix was finally complete.

Or so I thought . . .

Chapter Twenty:
Destroy the Dogs.

"Out of suffering have emerged the strongest souls."

- **Khalil Gibran**

It was the summer of 2000. I was home with my parents. I had left him and was on my way to divorce. My husband realized he was down to the last of his arsenal. Even his scary, little gun scheme didn't work. I had found a job in another state and would be leaving Texas for good.

My husband called, knowing I was back with my family. He knew I was helping my father with his recovery, which provided him with a perfect opportunity to drop a bombshell on me. Since I was never coming back to him, he was going to put both of our beautiful and loving dogs to sleep.

His false logic and thinly-veiled threat was that there would be no one there to look after them when he was off flying all around the world so why have them suffer. They would have no quality of life and it would not be fair to them. Why was it, I wondered, that he never offered to have me put to sleep or help me commit suicide when I too had no quality of life as a result of him being there?

As soon as I heard these words, fear cut through me like a bolt of lightning. I wondered if he made this suggestion just to get one more stab into me, leaving a scar he damn well knew would never heal.

I told him if he felt this way about it, I would take the dogs, buy a house in the Midwest and start my life over. A new house. A new job. A new community. A new beginning. Everything would be a fresh start and the dogs could still live with someone they knew and could adapt to different surroundings.

At the end of July, I was still living in my parents' house. My husband called to tell me our divorce was final. We had talked ahead of time about how we were going to split everything, and since there were no children to discuss or forms of child maintenance to be paid, it was a pretty cut-and-dry affair. He bought me out of our house and sent a settlement check. I could have been the spiteful "cunt" he had painted me to be all those years and taken his pension and insurable earnings hand-over-fist. However, as I had been living like a refugee under his command for so long, I wanted nothing to do with it. I didn't want to have any strings attached to him. The days of being his marionette had finally come to an end.

At the beginning of August, I finished classes I had been taking to keep my mind off things and flew down to Texas. These would eventually lead to my Master's Degree in teaching. He never allowed me to take any classes when I was with him. He didn't have a college degree so this was a point of contention with him.

A friend was waiting for me and my mother at the airport to help me bring my furniture and other belongings back. We rented a truck and went to my apartment. I hired two laborers to help us. We emptied it completely and didn't have time to organize things so neither of us had a bed to sleep on that last night.

The next morning, we took the truck over to my ex's house and picked up the last of my belongings. He was there waiting for me and was both pissy and edgy. My mother didn't want to come into the house, which gave him time to air his grievances about this to me. He bluntly stated he was going to tell her the same to her face. I didn't blame her for doing so as she did not want to be involved in any direct confrontation.

All of my belongings were packed up. He stayed inside the house and did not follow through with his threat. It was a surreal moment to finally and forever leave the man I had married and known for ten years. I had no feelings for him, yet I wanted to give him a goodbye hug. I didn't, though, because I knew from his body language this would have sent him into a blind rage. But even after how he had treated me all those years, and even though he was now my ex-husband, I still had a heart to try and let him know there was hope and that he might find love again – not with me, but perhaps someone down the line after he had done some serious soul-searching.

I wasn't able to see past or beneath his surface behavior when I was absorbing it and struggling to survive, but from the distance my freedom gave me, I no longer saw a raging psychopath. All I saw standing in the driveway watching me leave was a lost, lonely, sad human being, a boy in a man's body.

As we drove to my apartment, I wondered what happened in his childhood that had twisted his character so much. He was always too strong – or what he thought was strong - to talk about it so I never knew. As I watched the wind stirring the trees from my window, I also mourned the loss of the opportunity I might have had to help him recover from his past and be happy, had he allowed it.

I brought our dogs to the moving van and they moved back to the Midwest with me. I kept them both until the day they died of old age. Neither of his wishes - to destroy the dogs or to destroy me – were granted. We all survived and had the scars to show for it. Ten horrific, sadistic years rotting in hell. There is no other way to describe it.

Thirteen months later, he remarried to someone I believe was a mail order bride. He had quickly climbed back up on his horse and found someone who, I was told, didn't speak English, couldn't drive a car, didn't know anything about American culture, and had nowhere to run to get away from him. This was someone he could totally control. She walked straight into the nightmare I had just awoken from.

Basically, the bastard shook hands with the devil and got himself one hell of a good deal.

Chapter Twenty-One:
Emancipation.

"There is a crack in everything. That's how the light gets in."

- **Leonard Cohen**

At this point, I was totally free of my ex husband, living in harmony in Midwest America. It was harmony in the most basic sense of the word – lack of conflict. When anyone has walked the path I did for so many years, anything else is harmonious.

I had a new job. In fact, the whole world felt new. But as much as everything usually looked wonderful on the surface, there were still moments when I had to undergo a kind of self-exorcism to try to kill the demons that remained inside my head. This included his voice and the degradation of my personal character planted by him every day during those ten grueling years. He had programmed me to see myself as a failure, a worthless fuck, a stupid, pathetic, dumb cunt and, overall, a useless bitch.

I sold my car so I was unable to bring my dogs anywhere. Being a single woman was horrendous. I was discriminated against by car salesmen who thought it was improper for me to buy another vehicle without having a husband to sign for me. I lost approximately seventy percent of my total income at a time when I was trying to make purchases to better my life.

Trying to purchase a home wasn't easier, either. The banks slammed their doors in my face. I was a single woman coming off a divorce. The abuse continued. Although successful due to my own determination, I went from a 3100 square-foot house to a 615 square-foot one. I was being punished under a whole new framework and left thinking, "Whatever happened to humanity?"

I went to another bank. After explaining my situation for the umpteenth time, it was as if a miracle was occurring. The bank representative

At Least He Wasn't Hitting You...

with whom I spoke chose to not stone me to death as others had attempted, but instead said there was a loan out there for me and he was going to find it. He worked hard and got me a loan, but it came with a much higher interest rate. However, he added that the bank had a clause which stated that if my payments were made on time and there were no issues for at least a full year, they would consider knocking my interest rate down. I worked hard to do so and achieved not only one but two reductions in my interest rate.

One day I was at school and a child was giving me a lot of grief. I paused for a moment, angry not at the child but at my ex-husband because I was now battling life on my own. As much as I had desired and sought my freedom, I was mad at him for putting me in this position and not being a better husband. Had he been one, I would have remained by his side and tried to have children. If I couldn't, I would have sought to adopt children to give them a chance at life and not one spent in poverty or without loving parents.

Yet this was difficult because the voices in my head kept telling me I did not deserve to be here and should be back in my place, by his side, and under his control.

I gave it all I had, working a full-time job while pursuing a Master's Degree in teaching.

To this day, I continue to do battle with the demons in my mind, trying to regain a sense of who I was prior to marrying my oppressor.

Even though he wasn't hitting me, I was determined to get back on to my feet without his financial support.

Emancipation is on the horizon, but it has not been an easy journey for me. It continues to be an agonizing process. I am free physically but the heart and mind have their own timetable.

Closing

"If you walked away from a toxic, negative, abusive, one-sided, dead-end low vibrational relationship or friendship – you won."

- **Aisha Mirna**

I still have vivid memory of everything that happened, even though some of the abuse described in this book goes back twenty to thirty years. The memories do not simply disappear though I am hopeful that the worst part of my life is now behind me.

Sometimes I'm still amazed by the sheer amount of shit I plowed through yet am here to talk about. That I survived it is nothing short of a miracle. I could have been swallowed up by the monster years ago. I suppose the Creator had bigger plans for me that have yet to come forth. Perhaps part of that plan is putting these words to paper and telling my story because many women have their voices silenced before they can get out of their situations. I hope this story will demonstrate to someone struggling through a similar situation that I am not a cunt or any of the other things he tried to convince me I was, and neither are you the names your abuser is calling you.

I struggle with saying that brutal and degrading word. I guess being on the receiving end of such words countless times per day made me question a lot of things, including my sense of self, and if I was what he said I was. I know it is not true, but deprogramming myself, trying to unravel my thoughts, feelings, and intricate fibers of my very being to remove the vicious slurs that were carefully programmed into me has been an uphill battle.

I know this is going to take an awful lot of time, but my healing journey began when I left that marriage.

I remarried a wonderful, gentle soul. He taught me to love again. We were companions and friends who shared the gift of life without hate. Even though he is no longer here, he became and remains a part of my healing journey, as has sharing the words within these pages with you . . .

"I owe myself the biggest apology for putting up with what I didn't deserve."

- **lessonslearnedinlife.com**

Bruised and Battered

"If the wounds on her heart and the bruises on her soul were translated on her skin, you wouldn't recognize her at all."

- **Verona Q**

At the beginning of this book, I promised to tell the story of a dear friend of mine. This was first featured in my personal memoir titled, **Through the Eyes of a Belfast Child:** *Life. Personal Reflections. Poems.*

As you have read and will also now come to see, the beautiful lady who asked me to write her personal memoir has experienced similar yet quite different forms of abuse at the hands of her tormentor.

To this day, I do not know if my friend for whom this next piece was written is alive or dead. As mentioned previously, her abuse was often endured by way of a horrendously brutal, sexualized nature: repeated anal rape. This occurs at the hands of her partner when he

At Least He Wasn't Hitting You...

sees another man looking in her direction. She is naturally beautiful and an amazing soul, but like any other human, is underserving of what her body has been subjected to countless times.

This is her story . . .

After moving to Canada, while speaking with several girls at school who became good friends after getting over their not-so-secret crush on my accent, I could never really comprehend why they stayed with their abusive boyfriends. Their stories shared a consistent theme –their boyfriends would get drunk or high and then abuse them verbally. One of these young women was also abused mentally when her boyfriend would ask her repeated questions but slightly change them each time to get her to say what he wanted to hear her say, not the truth she was already speaking.

Antagonistic emotional abuse was used by telling her she was not good enough and that if he left her, no man would ever want to be with her as she was already "well used" and no one would want "leftovers" or "sloppy seconds."

Other forms of abuse were spiritual in nature, slowly ripping out the very soul of the young lady while making her feel worthless in every way, and only allowing her to have happiness as seen through his eyes. If he was happy, then what was she complaining about?

Last was the physical abuse that came in a variety of degrading forms, including sexual.

When they would disclose details of their relationships or seek my advice, I would often ask my female school friends why they chose to stay with their boyfriends who caused them so much pain and grief. It was a mystery to me why they would remain on the receiving end of such abusive behavior. I was surprised when their answers were always: *"I love him."*

My response was almost scripted, too:

"When you love someone, you do not treat him or her like they are nothing to you, no matter who is giving the abuse and who is on the receiving end of it."

At Least He Wasn't Hitting You...

Regardless of the advice given, my friends who had the courage to share often went back after an apology was received from their abuser, only for the cycle to start all over again the following week.

While in university, I took a family violence course in human ecology. I argued with one of my professors why the term rape is now referred to as sexual abuse. Rape is rape, I contended, no matter how one tries to define it - an act of complete victimization, degradation, and demoralization of a body, mind, and soul. I struggled with this issue. Due to the politically sensitive world we now find ourselves living in, we have begun desensitizing such an incredibly destructive action by adding an all-encompassing label.

There are many women who abide by traditional perspectives and follow a patriarchally defined lifestyle that may not be by choice. The same principle applies to those who find themselves in abusive relationships and seemingly have reasons to excuse their partner's actions.

"I upset him, so he got angry."

"If I just cooked his meal the way he likes it, he would never have called me those names."

"If I could only do more to make him happy, maybe he would love me the way I know he does deep down."

These are not excuses but mindsets that become almost permanent in nature for someone who has been repeatedly abused for many months or years and may not realize she has been programmed to respond in one manner or face consequences. As miserable as it may be, there are those who feel this is their lot in life and can do nothing about it.

It boils down to the cycle of violence theory that can be found in any human ecology course or textbook. However, those holding the power in any relationship are nothing without their partner, who unknowingly maintains a perfect imbalance.

Where would any of us be without the nurturing love and care that a woman provides in bringing us into this world? Without

At Least He Wasn't Hitting You...

women, our lives are not possible. With today's technology, and if women so choose, life could continue through the preservation of donated sperm. Using ultrasound technology, they could abort every male fetus until such a time they are needed. The course of history could certainly be very different.

Unfortunately, I have friends who have suffered in silence for years from abuses much like those contained in this book. They, along with others I do not know, feel that they have made their decision and must live and die by them. They are terrified to leave their abusers after years of psychological trauma. Their self-esteem has been devastated for so long, they feel completely worthless and undeserving of a better life.

I have a friend who has been molded to follow a regimented routine. She panics constantly in case she forgets one of her assigned actions. She has been called some of the most degrading and humiliating names a woman could ever endure, even after bearing two children who she raised alone for her partner.

She is not allowed to answer the phone or have any friends. She is not allowed to have a driver's license and is brought to work and picked up again to make sure she comes home to take care of the house and all else assigned to her. When she cries or falls to pieces from what her life has become and how she is treated, she is degraded that much further. If another man looks in her direction, she is punished when she gets home and reminded that only "he" has the right to look at her, even though she never acknowledged the gesture to begin with.

I am dedicating this updated version of my original poem to my same dear friend. Sadly, after twenty-five or more years of being trapped in her own hell, she continues to suffer in silence. To those women who have gone through years of abuse in past or current relationships. I dedicate this in the hope it brings some form of light to your stories and all you have gone through so that you may

At Least He Wasn't Hitting You...

recognize the signs of abuse and hopefully find help before you become fully disconnected from the support networks that are available. You are not alone. There is help!

Bruised and Battered

Welcoming him home from work,
She promised his favourite meal.
Offered a kiss before she cooked,
A dish of breaded veal.

It wasn't what he wanted,
Telling her to get out of his face.
He'd already had a rough day,
Plenty more work yet to chase.

She stated her apology,
And offered to make things right.
Sweetly she asked, "Will you join me,
In a bubble bath tonight?"

At Least He Wasn't Hitting You...

His response, as sharp as daggers,
"I've so much more to do!
Countless deadlines to meet,
Wasted dollars supporting you."

"Baby, you know I miss you," she sobbed,
"We never share quality time.
Is loving you deeply as I do,
Such a terrible crime?"

"What's wrong with you?" he screamed,
"Will you quit annoying me?
Once again you're under my skin,
Making me so very angry!"

"But honey, I love you so much!" she did cry,

"When not with you, I'm sad.

I only wanted to ensure your happiness,

I didn't mean to make you mad."

His rising hand, it slapped her face,

She fell like a lump of lard.

"Oh baby, can't you see I'm sorry,

I didn't mean to hit you so hard."

Her crumpled body upon the floor,

Her rosy cheek did sting.

Her trembling hand covering the bruise,

Left there by his high school ring.

At Least He Wasn't Hitting You...

Kneeling down onto the floor,
As he looked her in the eye.
"Baby, I really didn't mean it this time,"
One hand upon his fly.

She knew his sorrow meant nothing,
As her head began to throb.
He grabbed a handful of golden hair,
Her mouth began to bob.

"Baby, you know I really do love you,
When you take good care of me."
He would not let go of his grasp,
Until she had finished he.

Paralyzed by all her fear,

She asked, "Baby, did that feel good?"

Hoping just as she always did,

Her deed would lighten the mood.

"That makes things so much better,

Let's continue on with our day.

Good thing you know what best for you,"

He muttered while walking away.

As she rose up from the floor,

She prayed that it would end.

"Some day when I will find the strength,

My broken heart will mend."

At Least He Wasn't Hitting You...

Sitting back down at his desk,
His actions now in the past.
"Hey, when am I getting my dinner?
You'd better make it real fast."

She went to fix his plate,
And brought to him his meal.
"How did you know what I wanted?" he asked,
Upon seeing the breaded veal.

Many years have since passed,
Her heart remains broken and shattered.
Her pain hidden behind a fractured smile,
Her face still bruised and battered.

An Unexpected Visitor from the Grave.

"You will forever own a piece of me that I can never take back."

- **Unknown**

Date: July 24, 2018. Time: 23:21 hours.

Before explaining the meaning behind the title of this chapter and the note above with the timestamp, which was recorded as this all unfolded, I would like to mention a section from my last book that applies to the subject at hand. That book, **Four Green Fields**, is a memoir co-authored with two fellow Irish authors. In it, I told the story of the events leading up to my mum's untimely passing. To quote that section:

> *"We are given signs from those who have already departed this world. A week before, while sitting on my bed, and after having returned from visiting my mum, I saw my*

At Least He Wasn't Hitting You...

grandparents and my mum's two brothers standing at the foot of it. My granda had passed away in 1971. My uncle passed in 1987; my other uncle in 1988, and finally my granny in 1992, which was when I returned home for the first time after being away for seven years. I did not welcome their presence with open arms but swore at them and demanded to know why they were there. I was defiant and told them they were not taking my beloved mum. As much as I loved seeing their faces again, I shouted it was not her turn and asked for them go back to where they came from. I really didn't have a choice, for they came to release her from her suffering and needed me to prepare myself. My protests did not account for anything; it would not have been fair to my mum to prolong her suffering. Who was I to question why it was her time to venture into new beginnings, a new life, and a new adventure?

As you now know, my co-author and I have written about things happening for a reason, even if they cannot be explained or attempts are made by cynics to discredit them."

In light of the above, who was I to question another spiritual event that was about to occur while writing this book for the beautiful lady, who has been unbelievably and tremendously courageous in telling her story.

I had done my usual routine, working during the day as a social worker and supervisor in the field of child and family services. Immediately thereafter, I went to start my second job as a manager at a local family dining restaurant.

After wrapping up most nights around eleven P.M., I would make my way home and take my place in the exact same reclining spot on my couch, as I did every night since I started writing this story. Then I would set up my laptop, place a phone call to the subject of this book, and start writing for what I hoped would be a maximum of one hour. This was usually around eleven thirty or eleven forty-five P.M., but some nights went right though until two A.M. before I finally passed out from exhaustion, only to start the same routine all over again a few hours later.

The only thing out of the ordinary on this day was that I had driven home during my lunch hour to pick up some supplies for my son for his hockey practice later that evening.

Arriving at my house, I immediately noticed there was a package in my mailbox from a fellow Irish author who lives across the globe. Since I was in my usual mode of rushing around and had a million things to do, I placed the package on the countertop in the kitchen but did not get a chance to open it there and then. I thought I would do this later in the evening if I got home earlier than I normally do.

The story that was discussed and written that evening happened to be 'Pregnancies and

Miscarriages'. Aside from the graphic details, anguish and vicarious trauma I personally experience when I write, which now includes the book you are holding. This was nothing out of the ordinary whatsoever. It had been the same routine night after night for me. My house was set at about seventy-five degrees Fahrenheit, or just over twenty-three degrees Celsius. I sat in a pair of denim shorts and a golf shirt with a cup of tea beside me to help me stay awake. The wear and tear of working day and night, along with writing and publishing books in succession of one another, was beginning to take a personal toll. Although many of my colleagues are worried about me taking on so much at once, I refuse to burn out. There are stories to be told.

As Edna St. Vincent Millay's poem goes . . .

My candle burns at both ends;
It will not last the night;
But ah, my foes, and oh, my friends—
It gives a lovely light!

I wrote this book by taking notes rapidly as the subject told her story to me in riveting detail. From this, we developed the chapter headings. Other changes occurred dynamically while we were locked in deep discussion, or when one of us suddenly suggested something that stuck. In any case, it has been an interesting process and an enriching experience.

Next, I would simply sit and listen to try and get an idea as to what is going to be presented and how the chapter is going to unfold. Once ready, I allowed my fingers to write and was usually met with relaxed tones of breathing from the other end of my phone. If clarity was needed, I asked for it and kept tapping away on the keys until the story came together and had the proper feel and flow to it. From there, I would read the entire text back to this young lady and usually find myself apologizing profusely in advance as I knew what was going to be said from what she had already told me.

One night, I was quite shocked when she told me the way I was writing her story is was "beautiful." I thanked her for the compliment but, I questioned this as there is nothing beautiful about the content I have captured within these pages. There is nothing beautiful about having to read each chapter back to her, emphasizing each vicious remark she endured from her abuser.

For me, this has been nothing short of appalling. In social histories I'm given as a social worker, I read about incomprehensible trauma to the human body and spirit, and as troubled as I always am by them, especially when they involve children under my watch, I found myself struggling to write the condescending and cutting words of brutality spoken to the person behind this book. She assures me this is okay because she lived this experience and knows full well that my voice is telling her story, not her husband's. And though she told me not to worry when I told her I was concerned she might feel, through telling her story, that she was reliving the abuse all over again, it has become a delicate balance for me.

As I sat and captured the events of the D&C and was entering into the paragraph about the removal of the unborn fetus from her womb, I heard a scream from the other end of the phone followed by panicked gasps. I asked if she was okay but there was no answer. I heard another scream before she said *"Oh my God"* a few times in a state of complete fright.

I immediately thought she was having a heart attack or stroke. I asked again if she was okay. I was not prepared for her response or what was about to happen.

"He's here."

I responded, *"What? Who there's? What's going on? Are you okay?"*

"He's here. He hasn't been here for a while. He's in the master bathroom where he always appears and is lighting it up. He has never stayed this long before. There is a bright, blinding light coming from my bathroom. Oh, God."

Again, I asked if everything was okay as I had no idea who she may have been referring to or what she was seeing. I seriously had no clue what was going on until she said her deceased husband was standing in her bathroom. He had come back to visit and check in on her a few times before. This begins as him coming forth as an orb of light which starts off very slowly and glows for a short second or two before disappearing again. This time was going to be different. And it directly involved me.

Two years ago, I was back home in Northern Ireland with my daughter, son, and niece. We had gone over for a holiday for two weeks before taking one extra week in Croatia for the wedding of my cousin. Part of this trip involved bringing the ashes of my beloved sister back to Ireland. Her goal was to return home for the last time before the Acute Lymphoblastic Leukaemia she had been diagnosed with became worse and prevented her from traveling. She was in remission briefly prior to this trip and had planned to go over as she had

At Least He Wasn't Hitting You...

not been back since we left thirty years earlier. Sadly, she never did make it.

My niece brought some of my sister's ashes over for her mummy's best friend and her husband to keep, so my sister made it home but not in the form she wanted to.

I was driving down to Larne with these same friends, who were not only dear friends to my sister but a cherished part of our family circle. My sister and her best friend were inseparable while growing up together in Belfast prior to our immigration to Canada. We were on a hilly back road. I was in the front passenger seat with the fellow to my right driving, and his wife in the back seat. I brought up some memories of how my sister and her best friend were up on the Cave Hill one day when two fellas suddenly appeared out of nowhere on motorized dirt bikes. They began to circle my sister and her best friend. As uncomfortable as this was at the time, they began dating after we immigrated from Ireland. They went on to become wife and husband and had a beautiful family. We laughed about this.

As we continued driving along, and while the story unfolded further, the fella began giggling only to suddenly express a look of pure shock while letting out exasperated yelps:

"Flippin' hell. Oh my God. What the heck is happening? Flippin' heck. WOW!"

When I turned my head to look, moans of sheer panic and fear encompassed every fiber of his being! It was as if he had seen a ghost.

I was in the front passenger seat and knew exactly what was going on. He was wearing shorts and a t-shirt because was a blistering hot day. This was not normal for Belfast or where we were, out past Bally Carry. (*Game of Thrones* is filmed there). For thirty seconds, he gripped the steering wheel and held on to it for dear life, staring straight ahead of him. He could not move but could speak. The only way I can vividly describe this is he was lit up like a Christmas tree, yet his skin looked like that of a freshly-plucked turkey.

My sister had made her presence known and did what she could to grab his immediate attention. She sat inside him!

At Least He Wasn't Hitting You...

These friends had often heard me speaking about visitors who pop in from the spirit world and how they can let us know they are here with us. Over the years, I have explained to them about my work with the indigenous peoples in Canada and how I have submerged myself in the Anishinaabe culture. From this, they affectionately named me the **Irishinaabe.**

The beautiful worldview these people aspire to states that everything has a spirit, including human beings who are the two legged; trees who are the one legged; our four-legged friends, the animals, as well as birds, rocks, and plants which provide us with our medicines. To them, everything on this earth has a spirit. Other cultures either neglect to realize this or choose to turn a blind eye unless it is steeped in scientific merit.

The Anishinaabe perspective about women, which has been engrained in me, is another reason it has been so difficult to write this story. Women were revered in the indigenous traditions before they became colonized by white settlers, who imposed conditions like those the young lady for whom this story was written has experienced.

As my friend sat frozen, and in a complete state of shock and panic his arms and legs had massive welts on them, which looked like extremely enlarged goosebumps. And although the heat both outside and inside the vehicle was suffocating since there was no air conditioning, he was like pure ice to the touch. It was a feverish chill which he had never experienced before in his life! He did not know what the hell was happening to him. I laughed as everything unfolded. When he asked me why, I explained what was going on . . .

My sister's ashes had been brought home and we were talking about her memories from when she was young. The lad driving remembered what he and his mate were doing the day he ran into my sister and her best friend. I asked if he was going to take my niece up to the caves with his wife and re-enact those wonderful memories from years gone by. But since he was having a bit of fun and was laughing about it, I told him his unnaturally large goosebumps, physical paralysis and steeply dropping body temperature were all caused by my sister wanted to set the record straight and let him know she was keeping a wee eye on him.

To return to the evening of July 24, 2018, as I heard the screams of the woman behind this book and asked if everything was okay, I too suddenly experienced what I had seen happen to my sister's friend that day in Ireland, only my realization was she was being visited by her *second* husband, whom she had told me about prior to writing this book.

During one of the conversation we'd had to help me get a better understanding about her backstory, she shared with me a little bit about her second marriage; how loving this gentleman was. There was none of the brutal abuse, the power and control, the cutting remarks, or the plain ignorance and stupidity she had faced in her first marriage. The differences were night and day.

There was no need to consummate their marriage as it was not a sexual relationship. It was about two souls coming together for companionship. Love without hinderance. Without expectation. Without hateful remarks or abandonment when one needed the other. It was a love story which did not require the makings of a Disney fairy-tale, but instead one wherein two people could appreciate one another for who they were, not what they brought into the marriage.

At first, I had a hard time understanding this since marriage has been defined in the views of western society and ideology. In other countries, it too is seen as an act of ownership and in which the woman is expected to wait on her husband hand and foot or else be subjected to forms of abuse which is often accepted as being 'normal'. Many suffer in pure agony.

Yet this fella was determined to let his sweetheart know that he was here and not trying to *harm* her; that he is here is to *protect* her. This is where I come in.

As I was trying to ask her about what was going on in her home, I realized that what had happened to my sister's friend in Ireland was now happening to me. Her husband sat inside *me*!

At Least He Wasn't Hitting You...

My immediate response was peppered with a few expletives while I called out to let her know what was going on. Sure enough, the orb in her bathroom had vanished along with the

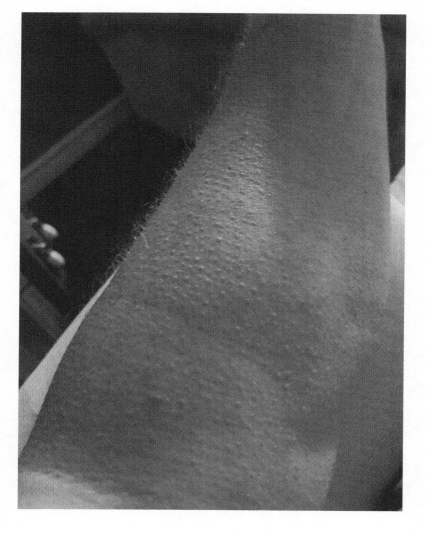

blinding light. Her husband made his way over because he knew I could relay to her what was going on, and not only in words. As I sat in my writing chair, it felt like someone was touching the sides of my face, trying to grab my attention. And believe me, he had it in full. This went from the right side of my face to causing an itching and tingling feeling in my head and then down to the left side of my face. My neck and shoulders were suddenly like ice, chilled to the bone even though it was over twenty-three degrees Celsius (seventy-five degrees Fahrenheit) in the house. All around my face was the same icy cold temperatures which usually comes with a spirit making its presence known. The hairs on were standing straight up only to be followed by massive goosebumps and chills shooting the length of my body. I wanted to prove this was happening and needed to find a way to show what was unfolding so I grabbed my phone and immediately started snapping photos.

What she told me next left me in a state of shock. I immediately said, "You're not gonna believe this." When I asked for the name of her husband, she said it loud and clear. Lo and behold, the name is the exact same as that of my fellow author who had sent me a copy of his latest book, which arrived that very

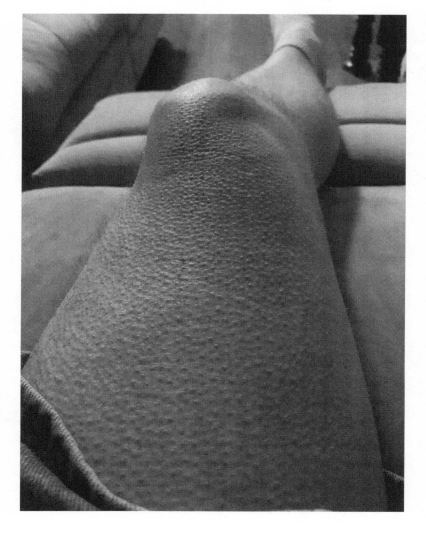

afternoon. It was then she realized the connection.

Her late husband had died exactly three years prior to this very date. I asked her to speak to him, as he was acknowledging her comments by sending signals through me. If something either of us said bothered him, he shot shockwaves of artic air down my body and lit me up with tremendously oversized goosebumps. These were on both sides of my body and over which I had zero control. Here are more photos from that night . . .

She spoke to him about unpleasantness she has experienced with his family since he passed. He was extremely angry about it and showed his displeasure by firing waves of cold air through my body yet again. She would go on to share absolutely everything she thought he did not know. Yet he acknowledged every heartbreaking and gut-wrenching story that she told.

I took the lead and asked her to speak to him as if he were here. She asked if I was frightened by all of this, to which I said I wasn't

At Least He Wasn't Hitting You...

as I'd had plenty of other supernatural experiences prior to this occurrence.

I asked her to speak about the day he passed. She told me they were in hospital

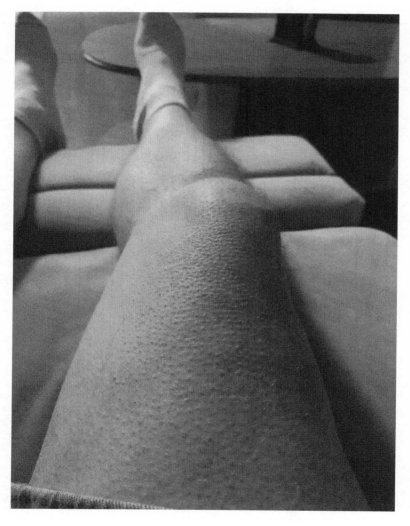

together. She held his hand and spoke to him, telling him how much she loved him and how happy the companionship they had established had made her. She held him and whispered comforting words until the moment his hand went limp, he exhaled his last breath, and he quietly slipped away from her. He acknowledged the memories he still held of his last moments on earth by squeezing me in a huge, bear-like hug, as if he were thanking her for making his passing lighter.

As she spoke about their happier memories together, the cold air which had penetrated my body suddenly left and became a warm flow as if pure adrenaline was now being injected directly into my veins.

In order to show her what was going on, I quickly formulated a plan. I told her I was hanging up the phone and would call her back for a video conference. As soon as the lines connected, I asked her to start asking this man questions. Before doing so, I stated she should tell me the name of her deceased husband and to speak directly to him so I could start

At Least He Wasn't Hitting You...

connecting with him from my 'side' of the energy portal he had opened.

She carefully watched all of this unfold through video, asking question after question

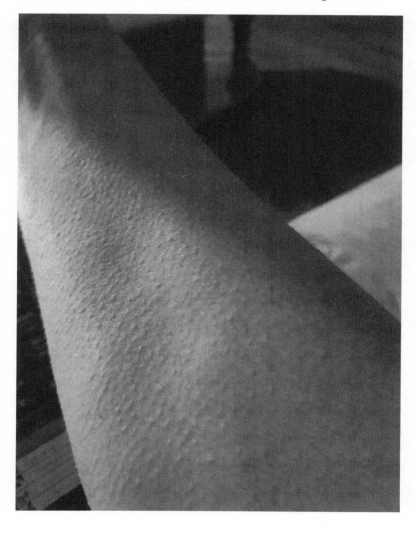

and waiting for his response. There were times nothing happened, which gave me a slight reprieve from the icy blasts shooting through my veins and along the tops of my skin. He was not answering those questions as they did not affect him. Everything was good and he was okay.

Next, I asked her to speak about her story and some of the events behind the chapter we were currently working on titled **Pregnancies and Miscarriages**. This had a tremendous affect on him, as he sent another round of sub-zero shockwaves along the nerve endings of every node in my body to demonstrate his displeasure to her.

I was being chilled to my bones and breathing in the deathly cold air associated with such a spiritual experience, but we had no choice but to accept the fact that I was the vessel he chose to communicate with her through.

This went on for over one hour before he returned to her bedroom and showed himself again as a blinding light in her bathroom. He appeared to her a total of four times that night in this manner, which he never did before. Still, it did not end there.

The following morning, I went to work and decided to tell a colleague about what had happened the night before. I was quite literally exhausted. My colleague could see this in my face as I did not get to sleep until the early hours of the morning. However, what I did not realize is that the deceased husband had kept the portal – me - open to stay connected to this world. I would learn late that night that he stayed with his sweetheart and was checking in with her from time to time that morning, just as he was visiting with me to show my colleague he was there in my office.

I was wearing jeans and a t-shirt. My colleague watched as I spoke and told her when I was going to light up, in full chills, and to watch my arms as it happened. This too lasted for over forty minutes as I explained everything in detail but did not provide the name of my friend other than to talk about her husband. Because I was wearing jeans, she was unable to see the goosebumps on my legs but did acknowledge that she too was getting a severe set of chills. She added that she had heard of events like this happening but had never witnessed it. As I talked about the different episodes I was experiencing or mentioned how badly my friend had been treated not only by her husband but by his family as well, it was almost as if her kind-hearted second husband was weeping tears of ice which flowed like glacier waterfalls over both of us. I then asked her if she recalled what I had written at the end of my first personal memoir but decided to share it all the same: shared with her something I had written in my first personal memoir:

> *"I once heard that I am not a human having a spiritual experience but that I am a spirit having a human experience. With that said, this is my life, in which I can help tell the stories of others who continue to define my worldviews through poems. This is my life, which I looked back upon through my own*

At Least He Wasn't Hitting You...

personal reflections. This is my life, as seen through the eyes of a Belfast child."

I still believe that to this day.

While putting this book together for my courageous friend who decided to take a chance and entrust me with her heart and soul, and openly discussed with me a chapter of her life she still struggles with, she showed tremendous bravery. But as is common with those who survive severe adversity, she was unaware of how courageous she is and seemed surprised when I told her so.

Each section has been discussed in excruciating detail, as she wanted to capture the very essence of what it was like to be a survivor in a relationship bursting with hatred. She wanted to capture the words and the snake strike effect they had when spoken . . .

"He hesitated before speaking, like a coiled snake, and when he spoke, I felt the words stab into me like the snake's fangs."

She hoped others in her position would recognize the expressions of malicious domination that was inflicted upon her without regard to the scars it left. And she wanted others to know that cruelty is not just a slap or punch, but that it can be emotional, mental, and even financial.

What I saw was her sheer determination to fight through second after agonizing second for her own survival, rising above, and continuing her battle to see another day so she could share her experiences with others, including me.

Looking back at my own life and the traumas I faced growing up during The Troubles in Northern Ireland and Canada, which I have openly shared in each of my five published books, she too expressed in explicit detail the human experience from not only *her* eyes but her heart and soul. A young lady from Midwest America, educated, who was never exposed to abuse or violence in any form until she muttered those fateful words, *"I do"*.

At Least He Wasn't Hitting You...

Regardless of the socioeconomic status she came from, and despite having a loving and supportive family behind her, one that never exercised the excessive disciplinary measures that were rampant when she was a child, her life changed for the worse anyway. As this story demonstrated, her first husband displayed inhumane actions and volatile language.

The vicarious trauma I personally absorbed while writing this book, and in reading it back to her, made me wish two things would have happened before she entered into that marriage – that a spirit from her own past had appeared to her and forewarned her of the misery that lay ahead of her if she married that man, and that instead of saying "I do" at the altar, she would have said, "I don't!"

The world is a mysterious place and humanity makes new discoveries every day. One thing I have been left wondering from writing this book, however, is this - after we have completed this human journey of life, is there some way we can take the hindsight gained from our experiences and turn them into foresight for our loved ones?

Her life changed again, as did mine when her second husband decided to help her understand he is here with her. She never was alone, even when he took his final breath. He's been with her all along, an unexpected visitor from beyond the grave, providing her with the indomitable strength and pure determination needed for her to put this story together with me.

If this book were to be written in this reverse perspective, she would have been in a much better position, but then her story would have never been told. It is a catch twenty-two situation.

Her second husband has brought a spiritual awakening to her by using me as his vessel through several bone-chilling yet warming episodes one evening when he traversed heaven and earth to come to her side again. And I would be willing to wager that he will be the light she sees and walks to when her time is up, when she hears her name whispered in

At Least He Wasn't Hitting You...

the breeze and they are able to hold each other again.

She now has peace of mind and the comfort of knowing that when he appears in her bathroom as a glowing orb of light, she need not be afraid but only nurture his spirit and welcome his presence. Even if she never marries again, she has the solace of knowing that her second husband is by her side.

From the First Nations worldview, and as I have been taught by my indigenous mentors, I told my friend that she should honor the presence of his spirit by laying down tobacco.

Even if she never marries again, she will have pure comfort knowing that her second husband, the man who loved her for who she was and adored her companionship without asking questions or spitting hateful remarks in her face, walks beside and is watching over her by day and night. He is keeping his dearly beloved safe.

In closing, I am left to wonder how many other women have gone through a similar journey. How many women spent months, years or even decades not living the adventure of marriage but suffering the torture of it. How many women gained a post-secondary education they never asked for. How many women entered a relationship they thought would allow them to express themselves openly, share love freely, gain financial freedom, and start a family, only to have it all shot to hell by the wrong partner.

Is this not the dream of every young lady when she walks down the aisle? Does the thought of someday writing their own personal memoir of abuse and survival ever cross their minds before being pronounced husband and wife?

I have yet to hear the direct opposite of that patriarchal expression spoken:

"I now pronounce you woman and husband."

As I shared previously,

"In life, we all have a cross to bear and a very unique story to tell; we just hope that someone will take the time to listen."

In saying so, I thank you for taking the time to listen to *her* story, which may indeed be similar to the story you have waiting inside of you . . .

To end this book, and to honor the spirit of her beloved husband, protector and guardian angel, I am sharing a piece I composed in 1998 while standing at the foot of my granny's and granda's grave on a hill overlooking Belfast Lough. They are peacefully laid to rest within Carnmoney Cemetery, County Antrim, Northern Ireland but continue to watch over me every day.

Whispers in the Breeze

Realizing my innermost fears,
Choking back the steady stream of tears.
Not knowing your time had come,
Without you I feel so numb.

Just a whisper in the breeze,
Brought my world down to its knees.
The day that you were called away,
Paradise is where you now stay.

When the days do come to pass,
I call upon your bed of grass.
Comfort inside knowing you're there,
Looking up at my vacant stare.

At Least He Wasn't Hitting You...

The silence I exchange with thee,

Speaks volumes, I'm sure this you'll see.

My shadow casts across your grave,

While I stand so lonely, I stand so brave.

Now the days they seem so long,

In your arms is where I belong.

I close my eyes and hear you speak,

You call my name; my legs feel weak.

Together we promised that we would grow old,

We thought our happiness would never unfold.

I kneel at your feet with my head hung low,

Thoughts in my mind you already know.

Greg McVicker

This quality time with you I spend,

Will hopefully help my broken heart mend.

Feeling guilty when I turn to leave,

Returning home, I continue to grieve.

When my term approaches death,

Time to exhale one final breath.

I wonder if others will fall to their knees,

When my name whispers in the breeze.

At Least He Wasn't Hitting You...

Connect with the Author

In my work as a supervisor and social worker in the field of child and family services, I encounter a lot of terrible situations. I cannot begin to calculate how many times I swear under my breath or out loud. Human behavior presents extremely damaging revelations. Perpetrator's use stealthier approaches; self-serving policies and political ideology cause staff to quit while systems collapse. Money matters. Lives don't!

However, listening to this lady's story and writing this book for her shook even me. The most disturbing stories are captured in the chapters titled *Pregnancies and Miscarriages*, *Evil Task Master* and *Cold Hard Steel*. There was a massive knot in my stomach while trying to bring this all together.

I immediately noticed while promoting this book prior to its launch, and from the initial reader's reviews, that countless individuals have lived through similar experiences.

Abuse, regardless of its presentation, is like a cancer. As humans, none are immune to it. And just like cancer, none of us want it. Upon rearing its ugly presence, it takes hold in ways we never imagine. The more we ignore it, the darker our lives become, and the less likely it will be that we will go on living. The good news is help is never far away.

Do you have a story to tell?

I have been contacted by a few people asking to write their story, just as I have done for the inspirational lady whose voice stands behind this book. Thank you. I am honoured.

Thus, I would also love to hear your story. Only our Creator knows the wisdom and comfort that might come from another reading your words or how your story might help someone else discover that not only are there are others

At Least He Wasn't Hitting You...

who have walked in their footprints, there are those who can help!

If you are interested in connecting with me, please feel free to use one of the platforms listed below. I make every effort to respond to all enquiries within a timely manner and certainly look forward to hearing from you. Just know you're not alone.

Call the mental health center or a licensed therapist in your community. Reaching out is the first stage of healing. Take one step and one day at a time. Remember: breathe!

email:	gmcvicker70@gmail.com
facebook:	ThroughtheEyesofaBelfastChild
twitter:	@BelfastChild70 **#IAM**
Instagram:	belfastchildpublishing

Other Titles from Greg McVicker

Through the Eyes of a Belfast Child:
Life. Personal Reflections. Poems.

First Edition - May 2014
Second Edition - November 2017

ISBN: 978-1-7751622-6-1
(Softcover)

978-1-7751622-7-8
(eBook)

"This is totally fantastic! Even the wee poems were such a pleasure to read. This is something I'd read again and again. Above all, I'm sure your mammy is looking down on you with such pride and love. I have never read such beautiful words written by anyone to describe their mum as you have. The feelings are there, but putting them into words is something else. I actually filled up reading some parts, a wee mixture of smiles and tears. I'm sure that anyone else who reads this will react exactly the same. Not only have you put a lot of hard work and time into this, you've written this with your heart."

- **Teresa McAuley**
  Belfast, Northern Ireland.

At Least He Wasn't Hitting You...

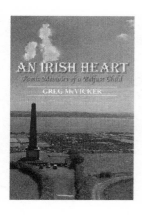

An Irish Heart:
Poetic Memoirs of a Belfast Child

First Edition:
October 23, 2017

ISBN: 978-1-7751622-0-9
(Softcover)

978-1-7751622-1-6
(eBook)

"The book and poetry are so special. It is a heartwarming, disturbing and complex view of how things were from Greg's journey from his beloved 'Norn Iron' to Canada, and beyond, with great principles at work in himself, and from many others whom he met along the way. It incorporates spiritual, psychological, and political dimensions. Greg's journey proves that despite cruelty and terrible conditions, human beings can somehow get through the worst that life throws at us with love, support, and friendship, which re-ignites 'the will to live'. His Irish, Canadian and humanitarian spirit looms large through his writing and his beautiful poetry. It is profound, funny, and moving. It deserves to be read carefully to the end, in a spirit of meditative reflection in order to fully appreciate the character of the man and his journey."

- **Gerry Rogers**
  Edinburgh, Scotland.

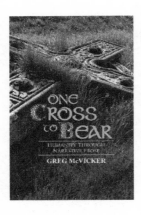

One Cross to Bear:
Humanity Through Narrative Prose

First Edition:
October 23, 2017

ISBN: 978-1-7751622-2-3
(Softcover)

978-1-7751622-3-0
(eBook)

"Using his distinctive style of storytelling by way of stanza and prose, Irish Poet and Author Greg McVicker dives headfirst into the turbulent cycle of life. In "One Cross to Bear", his latest collection of poetry, he takes us on a whirlwind journey of his years growing up in his native Northern Ireland, up to the present day in Canada. Poems such as Belfast City Asylum and Everlasting Homesickness paint a vivid picture of growing up in war-torn Belfast, and the pain he endured at being torn away from all that he knew in order to start a new life in a safer but foreign land. Greg writes unashamedly from the heart, reaching out to his readers and carrying them along the waves of an emotional tsunami. I have no doubt that these poetic stories have and will continue to affect untold numbers of individuals throughout their lifetime."

- **J.P. Sexton,**
  Author of:
  'The Big Yank *Memoir of a Boy Growing Up Irish.*'

At Least He Wasn't Hitting You...

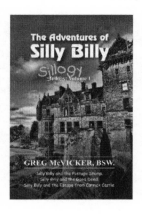

The Adventures of Silly Billy:
Sillogy: Volume 1.

First Edition:
November 2017

ISBN: 978-1-7751622-4-7
(Softcover)

978-1-7751622-5-4
(eBook)

The Adventures of Silly Billy are based on the true-life childhood experiences and misadventures of Irish author, poet and storyteller, Greg McVicker. Each story takes place within his community of Newtownabbey, County Antrim, Northern Ireland. This book is suitable for children of all ages and adults who wish to revisit their childhood!

"Do you know what I love about your books? They are written from a time when there were no computers and no electronic games. Childhood was simple then, although it wasn't simple for us. In saying that, Greg uses his personal experience of being a child with subtle differences in Northern Ireland. Combining humour, 'Norn Ireland' dialect and creativity, Greg gives us an insight and reminder of being a child. Young or old, you will enjoy this unique insight into children in 1970's Norn Ireland."

-   **Gráinne Clancy**
    Dublin, Ireland.

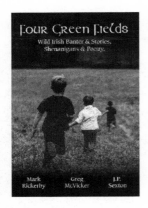

Wild Irish Banter & Stories, Shenanigans & Poetry.

First Edition:
July 1, 2018

ISBN: 978-1-989053-06-5
(Softcover)

978-1-989052-07-2
(eBook)

Welcome Home to the Emerald Isle!

"The authors behind Four Green Fields, which include Greg McVicker, Mark Rickerby, and J.P. Sexton, have gone above and beyond on their promise to bring us "wild Irish banter and craic." They have literally thrown open the doors of their collective closets and introduced us to the family skeletons, put flesh back on their bones and made them dance! Not only do we get a glimpse into the wacky world of their Irish upbringing, but we are introduced to fathers, grandfathers and uncles - utterly devoid of any sense of political correctness - who at times went about their daily lives oblivious to the havoc they wreaked around them, but at other times knew full well the embarrassment they were causing their families."

From the Author to The Voice

To my wonderful, inspirational and extremely courageous friend...

Thank you for placing your full trust and belief in me asking me to write your book. Thank you to all the phenomenal individuals around the world who have provided the early reviews of this book. It was not an easy task. Their words have left me in awe and sincere appreciation.

I have spoken about my struggles in each of my books about a childhood trauma. One of the biggest was the day a "teacher" told me, "You will never amount to anything." I will not use this person's name because she does not deserve to be mentioned.

I finally feel as if I have exorcised the demon of my primary school learning years at the front pages and back cover of this book have helped me put them to rest even more.

To the teacher who tore me and other kids to shreds and destroyed our self-belief of ever being someone who could achieve their dreams and goals if they tried, I can finally say *you* lost. I have done much more than you ever thought possible. I have achieved my dreams and goals. People know my name and, unlike you, they believe in me!

How dare you enter a position of trust only to then try to destroy a child, demolishing their self-worth and dignity as you did to me for over forty years because of your own venomous tongue and cutting words.

I have finally proven to myself that **#IAM** someone and, contrary to your hideous perceptions of me, I have become something.

#IAM Greg McVicker, the proud son of Catherine and Charles McVicker. I can again stand tall, hold my head high and say I did it!

#IAM a father of two beautiful and loving children who have achieved incredible success in their own young lives because they were and continue to be supported and encouraged, just as my mum and dad have done for me.

#IAM a social worker, one who has an established career of fighting tooth and nail by passionately advocating for those who are marginalized and are quite often seen as being disposable humans within systems and policy.

It has taken forty years for me come to this realization, but I have finally beaten your selfish descriptions in which I would never amount to anything. Again, I have proven that you were and are so wrong.

The time has come in which I start believing in myself! I say the same for every child, now adults and whose ages are within a few years of my own. You single-handedly sacrificed our dignity all because of the physical, mental, emotional and verbal abuse you served up to us all in your evil, tormented classroom.

Once and for all, I have silenced the voice in my head which belongs to you. You can keep it, for it does not deserve to take up space in my mind. This is your eviction notice!

For those of you reading this and struggling with self-worth, believe in yourself. Recognize your strengths and do not be afraid to tell yourself who or what you are just as I AM:

#IAM proud of myself.

#IAM proud of my abilities.

#IAM proud of my accomplishments.

#IAM an Irish Author, Poet, and Storyteller.

In saying this, much like the courageous voice behind this story for whom this book is written, my goals, dreams and aspirations are only getting started! Do not let anyone extinguish the spirit within your soul or tell you that you're not important. YOU ARE!

Remember: we enter this world with nothing and exit from it the exact same way. Live your life to the fullest but leave behind the gentlest footprint you can. The creation of your legacy starts with you; the story within you is just waiting to be written...

Greg.

At Least He Wasn't Hitting You...

25311462R00150

Made in the USA
Columbia, SC
06 September 2018